Beyond Data

Reclaiming Human Rights at the Dawn of the Metaverse

Elizabeth M. Renieris

The MIT Press

Cambridge, Massachusetts | London, England

The MIT Press would like to thank the anonymous peer reviewers who provided comments on drafts of this book. The generous work of academic experts is essential for establishing the authority and quality of our publications. We acknowledge with gratitude the contributions of these otherwise uncredited readers.

This book was set in ITC Stone Serif Std and ITC Stone Sans Std by New Best-set Typesetters Ltd. Printed and bound in the United States of America.

Library of Congress Cataloging-in-Publication Data

Names: Renieris, Elizabeth M., author.
Title: Beyond data : reclaiming human rights at the dawn of the metaverse / Elizabeth M. Renieris.
Description: Cambridge, Massachusetts : The MIT Press, [2023] | Includes bibliographical references and index. | Summary: "A Future Beyond Data aims to shift the conversation to an approach that centers people, not data, and draws on the international human rights framework. In response to the immersive, cyberphysical reality that is rapidly developing, this book argues for a more expansive interpretation of human rights, beyond rights to privacy or data protection, to address the complex array of threats and challenges posed by enveloping digital technologies"—Provided by publisher.
Identifiers: LCCN 2022017743 (print) | LCCN 2022017744 (ebook) | ISBN 9780262047821 (hardcover) | ISBN 9780262373418 (epub) | ISBN 9780262373425 (pdf)
Subjects: LCSH: Internet—Social aspects. | Big data—Moral and ethical aspects. | Human rights. | Data privacy. | Internet governance.
Classification: LCC HM851.R4575 2023 (print) | LCC HM851 (ebook) | DDC 302.23/1—dc23/eng/20220624
LC record available at https://lccn.loc.gov/2022017743
LC ebook record available at https://lccn.loc.gov/2022017744

10 9 8 7 6 5 4 3 2 1

Contents

Author's Note

Throughout this book, I frequently use the terms *data protection*, *data privacy*, *data security*, and *data governance* as well as *privacy*. I tend to use *data protection* and *data privacy* interchangeably, using the former more often in the context of European and European-inspired laws and regulations, and the latter more frequently in the context of the US legal framework. I also use *data governance* as an umbrella concept that encompasses all manner of laws and regulations that seek to regulate how data about people is collected, processed, and used, including data protection, data privacy, and data security–related laws and regulations. This language dominates the technology governance discourse.

In general, I use the term *privacy* to refer to an idea that is much older than data protection or data privacy—an idea that is rooted in constitutional and international human rights law, and much bigger and broader than what can be understood through the lens of data. Unfortunately, in the US context, *privacy* and *data privacy* are often used interchangeably, although they are not the same. In fact, as I argue throughout this book, privacy is increasingly being reduced to a technocratic, data-centric notion, eroding the power of its original conceptualization. Ultimately, I hope to shift the conversation away from its data-centric framing toward a more expansive view rooted in human rights.

Preface

In 2003, I was a sophomore in college when one of my classmates hacked into our internal residential house directories, scraped the student ID photos of female residents from their pages, and repurposed them for a website with the domain name facemash.com. The site pitted undergraduate women against each other, asking classmates to vote for the "hotter" of the two. Despite clearly violating several university information technology policies and causing an uproar among female student groups on campus, my classmate faced no disciplinary action and would go on to control one of the world's most powerful companies in the world. That classmate was Mark Zuckerberg.

For nearly two decades since, I have been steeped in conversations about data with everyone from lawmakers and policymakers to academics and researchers, engineers and CEOs, and even more recently, friends and family—discussions that usually revolve around companies like Facebook (now Meta), Google, and Amazon. As a data protection and privacy lawyer with more than a decade of experience across several continents, and an academic who also researches data governance frameworks, I often cannot escape thinking or talking about data (and now writing about it too, you might argue). But as a human being who recalls feeling deeply offended by my classmate's experiment, the data conversation never felt like it got to the heart of the matter or injuriousness of the experience.

And so this book is not about data, at least not at its core. Rather, it is about what lies *beyond* data. It is about recognizing that we have grown collectively obsessed with data, and that this obsession is a dangerous and unhealthy distraction from what's really at stake in relation to technological development—a distraction that Zuckerberg is all too happy to entertain, especially as he evangelizes a vision for a new virtual world known as the *metaverse*. It is about the dangers of understanding our relationship to technology, and anchoring our core governance strategies for it, from the perspective of data, examining how we got to this point in the first place, and mapping a new path forward.

This book is about reclaiming our power by remembering a time before data and imagining a future beyond it.

Prologue

I began this book in the spring of 2020 with the world facing its first global pandemic since an influenza outbreak claimed an estimated fifty million lives a century ago, at the end of the first world war. In response to the public health crisis spawned by a new viral pathogen (SARS-CoV-2) and resulting respiratory illness (COVID-19), countries around the world imposed curfews, lockdowns, and social distancing measures to keep people physically isolated. While historical letters and diaries from the early twentieth century reveal the deep isolation and loneliness of people with limited means of staying connected or entertaining themselves during the influenza outbreak,[1] modern technologies would play a prominent role in our lives during this twenty-first century pandemic.

Virtually overnight, life would migrate online for large swaths of the population as digital tools and learning apps replaced physical classrooms, videoconferencing technologies became our offices, and in-person doctor's visits migrated to telemedicine and telehealth services. Even judicial proceedings, congressional hearings, and intimate ceremonies such as weddings and funerals were conducted remotely. Cut off from cultural activities and social engagements, millions of people flocked to social media apps such as

TikTok, whose popularity surged to more than a billion users world-wide. Technologies kept us connected in a time of great disconnection, offering entertainment and escape (and for some, a glimpse of the promise and peril of a notional "metaverse").

But as the pandemic increased our reliance on these technologies, it also laid bare their vulnerabilities and shortcomings. The proliferation of remote tools for learning, working, and other activities, revealed the heightened potential for abuse of these technologies to monitor and surveil students, employees, and people in their own homes, while the introduction of pandemic-related tools and technologies to track and trace the spread of the virus and verify vaccinations led to zealous debates about the overreach of governments and large corporations alike in the lives of individuals and entire communities. As a result of pandemic-related supply chain disruptions, shortages of the semiconductor chips that power our digital tools and technologies slowed the production of essential supplies and threatened critical infrastructure. And social media platforms quickly flooded with dangerous mis- and disinformation about COVID-19, vaccines, and political developments. As just one vivid illustration of these effects, the United States held a widely contested presidential election and underwent a violent insurrection on its Capitol by those who refused to accept its outcome and who were galvanized through online channels such as Facebook.

The ever-expanding role of digital technologies in our lives, accelerated by the pandemic in such visceral ways, has also exposed the limitations of existing laws and regulations to effectively govern them, particularly laws focused exclusively on data. Fortunately, there are some changes on the horizon.

In February 2020, at the dawn of the pandemic, European Commission president Ursula von der Leyen unveiled a new digital strategy and far-reaching legislative package to match,[2] including a flurry of proposals for new regulations to promote cross-sectoral data sharing and innovation,[3] provide enhanced data access and portability for consumers,[4] and address the market power of online platforms,[5] as well as a comprehensive framework to govern artificial intelligence[6] and additional domain-specific regulations related to cybersecurity and other subjects.[7] As I write this, some of the proposed regulations have become law while others remain drafts under negotiation. Nevertheless, they represent Europe's first major overhaul and modernization of its laws to govern digital technologies in nearly two decades. And while not explicitly stated by lawmakers, the measures could move Europe away from a singular focus on data protection as a means of modern technological governance, at least to a degree.

Meanwhile, things have been far quieter in Washington, DC, with one major exception. After my manuscript went into production, the first bipartisan, bicameral, comprehensive privacy bill with a genuine shot of becoming law was introduced, after decades of stalemate and inaction on federal privacy legislation.[8] The law would grant individuals a host of rights familiar under other privacy laws and regulations, including rights related to the access, correction, deletion, and portability of data, as well as new rights in relation to misleading or manipulative user interfaces and targeted advertising. It would also require data minimization, only allowing entities to process covered data for specifically enumerated permissible purposes, prohibit entities from collecting, processing, or transferring covered data in a discriminatory manner, and impose certain duties of loyalty on entities processing data, among its other features.

While it was too late in the production of this manuscript to materially address these developments, it is important to at least acknowledge them here and address the extent to which they support my argument in this book, which is that we must go beyond data to protect people. Not only has the world changed dramatically since I began writing this book, but we are now also at an inflection point in our approach to technology governance, presenting either a unique chance to get this right or else a missed opportunity. If history is our guide, we should temper our expectations.

These measures are still largely focused on data, continue to presume a level of individual control, and are crafted for an oversimplified (and in some ways, obsolete) technological reality rather than the one that is imminent or rapidly emerging. Tellingly, the recitals to Europe's new draft data governance legislation proclaim, "Digital technologies have transformed the economy and society, affecting all sectors of activity and daily life. *Data is at the centre of this transformation.*"[9] As I argue throughout this book, one of the most fundamental ways we have gone wrong in our approach to technology governance is by repeatedly centering data over people, even when we purport to have a "human-centric" approach. While these European regulations are still new and untested, they are at risk of making the same mistake.

Moreover, Europe's new strategy repeatedly emphasizes innovation and data's economic value, while placing tremendous faith in the ability of technologies to protect individual rights. It highlights "techniques enabling privacy-friendly analyses on databases that contain personal data, such as anonymisation, pseudonymisation, differential privacy, generalisation, or suppression and randomisation," and encourages "the use of increasingly available technology that permits algorithms to be brought to the data and allow valuable insights to be derived without the transmission between parties or unnecessary copying of the raw or structured data themselves."[10] As I explain in this book, laws that focus on the confidentiality, privacy, and security of data, especially when achieved by technical means, are extremely vulnerable to manipulation and will not protect people from the kinds of threats to their dignity and autonomy that privacy seeks to guarantee. In fact, they risk creating a perception of safety, while sustaining harmful activities.

Although people are more aware of the potential risks and harms associated with new and emerging technologies, the chasm between their concerns and any realistic modicum of control over things continues to grow. Meanwhile, the law continues to embrace flawed notions of individual choice and control over their digital experience. For example, Europe's new regulations purport to give people more control over their experience on digital platforms through a similar paradigm to traditional privacy and data protection laws by mandating additional transparency and requiring platforms to introduce new user controls and options. The theory is that with enough transparency through robust notices and more detailed disclosures, individuals will be able to better adjust or calibrate their experience of algorithmically mediated processes, despite the fact that this theory or approach has not worked in practice regarding control over the uses or treatment of personal data, coupled with the exponentially increased complexity of AI and machine learning tools.

Even in the United States, where the new bipartisan draft federal privacy bill is being hailed by many as a great compromise, there are warning signs. Whereas industry has been uncharacteristically quiet on the bill, privacy professionals and advocates have been largely supportive of it, perhaps due in part to the sentiment that something is better than nothing. While these efforts are laudable and would certainly represent an improvement on the status quo, they nevertheless proffer an approach that is unsustainable (and it is unlikely that we will see the kind of political will and cooperation necessary to make another material overhaul in the foreseeable future). In fact, as one congresswoman describes it, the legislation is "a band-aid for the American people who are just fed up with the lack of privacy online."[11] But a band-aid can only ever stop the bleeding. And we desperately need something more enduring.

As I argue in this book, what we need instead is a broad human rights-based approach to technology governance. Nevertheless, I want to acknowledge the serious difficulties and challenges with proposing such a path forward, particularly at a time characterized by heightened geopolitical fracturing, economic turmoil, and unprecedented instability. As I write this prologue, Ukraine remains under the violent invasion of Vladimir Putin's Russian army, tensions are mounting between China and Taiwan, and decades-old ethnic conflicts are resurfacing in the Balkans and elsewhere. In short, human rights and the institutions needed to secure them are exceedingly vulnerable. But they are no less vital. In my view, human rights are the only meaningful and sustainable way forward. It is only when we begin with people, as human rights do, that we can better withstand the rapidly evolving technological landscape, even if we should eventually find ourselves at the dawn of the metaverse.

Introduction

At the dawn of 2020, it is estimated that we surpassed 44 zettabytes of digital data in existence.[1] That's 44,000,000,000,000,000,000,000 bytes of data, which is approximately forty times more bytes than there are stars in the observable universe. By the year 2025, the amount of data generated worldwide each day will be approximately 463 exabytes, which is nearly one hundred times more than all the words ever spoken by human beings since the dawn of time.[2] The exponential growth in data creation as more humans and machines come online has been dubbed a *data tsunami* by some industry experts.[3] While these numbers can be impossible to comprehend, there is no question that we are drowning in data.

And yet no one is quite sure what this data is. While we tend to think of data as facts or an abstract representation of some objective truths (the expression "the data doesn't lie" comes to mind), we struggle to find an apt metaphor to capture the role of digital data in modern life. The historical usage and evolution of the term *data* over the course of modern history paints a similarly complicated picture. As it turns out, we have never really been able to agree on what data is or what role it plays in our culture.

This elusive quality of data makes it an extremely vulnerable foundation for consensus building or norm setting. And yet the bulk of our approach to the governance of new and advanced digital technologies to date has centered on data—specifically laws and regulations that speak to the privacy, security, and confidentiality of *data*. In fact, the more challenges we face as technology evolves, the more we seem to tether ourselves to data as both the problem and solution to our problems.

As I argue in this book, this data-centric approach is putting us all at risk by distracting from the original aims of data protection—namely protecting people. In the chapters that follow, I will endeavor to explain where we are, how we got here, and where we should aspire to go next. But first, I return to this question: *What is data?*

What Is Data?

Data has largely evaded definition, rather being described indirectly by reference to something else, as evidenced by a flurry of metaphors for it. One of the most frequent characterizations is data as a form of property. While not the first to depict data as property, former Cambridge Analytica operative Brittany Kaiser, who also featured in the 2019 film *The Great Hack*, popularized the analogy when she launched an #OwnYourData campaign in its wake.[4] Calls to *own* or *control* data as property ratcheted up as the #OwnYourData movement was embraced by everyone from popular artist will.i.am to former presidential candidate Andrew Yang.

In the years after the Cambridge Analytica scandal, the number of *data as* ____ metaphors seemed to proliferate daily. Hearkening back to an earlier report from the World Economic Forum, a 2019 article in the *Economist* proclaimed data as the world's most valuable resource, leading many experts to describe data as the *new oil*, while others dubbed it the *new water*, *new air*, and even *sunlight*.[5] Comparisons have also been made to data as *labor, currency, nuclear waste*, and *asbestos*, among other toxic substances.[6] In her seminal work *The Age of Surveillance Capitalism*, Harvard scholar Shoshana Zuboff defines *data* as "the raw material necessary for surveillance capitalism's novel manufacturing process."[7]

But as artificial intelligence (AI) scholar Kate Crawford contends in the *Atlas of AI*, many of these metaphors, particularly those describing data as a kind of natural resource or raw material, represent an intentional rhetorical strategy by powerful institutions to characterize data as something abstract, inert, and non-human, rather than as something personal or intimate relating to the individual. For Crawford, this view is productive in the sense that "extraction is justified if it comes from a primitive, 'unrefined' source."[8]

In some ways, data is simultaneously all of these things and also none of them. Data is entirely contextual and dynamic, making it almost impossible to define. As we will see, trying to regulate *data* as such is like trying to regulate *technology* as if it had a common definition or clear contours—an exercise in futility.

Historical Origins of *Data*

Etymologically, the word *data* derives from the Latin word *datum*, meaning "a thing given" (the past participle of the Latin verb *dare*, meaning "to give"). The Latin term implied movement or transmutation—*data* not as something static, but as something fluid; not a fact, but a given. In modernity, the term was actually popularized by theologians and humanists before it was widely adopted by scientists and mathematicians, perhaps rather ironically as data has now taken on a kind of religiosity of its own. As historian Daniel Rosenberg puts it, "The *idea* of data—'data-ism' even— has become central to contemporary culture, to our understanding of our world, and ourselves."[9]

Rosenberg traces the modern usage of the word *data* to a seventeenth-century, Oxford-educated English cleric and theologian named Henry Hammond who published a series of letters and texts in which he used the term. In the spirit of its Latin etymology, Hammond used *data* to mean "stipulations" or "concessions," in the sense of things given or taken for granted in an argument, with no judgment about their veracity or truth. In fact, whether they were true or factual was immaterial, or irrelevant even. For Hammond, examples of data were that priests should be called to prayer or liturgy should be rigorously followed.[10]

The use of *data* as a rhetorical concept referring to things taken or stipulated "for the sake of" argument, versus for any inherent truth or veracity, would persist throughout the seventeenth century. Disciplines from theology to philosophy and mathematics used the term *data* to identify facts and principles that were agreed to be beyond argument based on self-evident principles, as was often the case in theology, or else simple argumentative convenience, as was common in algebra.[11] This notion persisted through at least the mid-eighteenth century when, for example, another Oxford-trained scholar studying magnetism used the term *data* to mean "axioms given prior to experimental investigation"—quite literally the opposite of facts.[12]

The rise of empiricism in the mid- to late eighteenth century transformed the usage of the term *data*, which would become more commonly used to refer to raw, unprocessed information extracted by investigation, more akin to facts gathered through observation and collection (of course, contradictions are inherent in the need to *extract* something that is presumably *raw*).[13] In other words, *data* came to be understood as the result of, instead of a premise for, investigation or inquiry—as something objective.

Just as this shift in meaning was taking place, the term would largely fall out of usage, going through a period of cultural latency that would last for nearly a century. When it reemerged in the mid-twentieth century, *data* came to be associated with quantified information structured, stored, and communicated through computational machines—the data that makes up bits and bytes. As Rosenberg explains, "*Data* first emerged as a tool for setting aside questions of ontology [and] re-emerged at the center of our general culture as it produced ontologies of its own."[14] In fact, the elusive and unintelligible nature of the term is perhaps partly responsible for its ongoing adaptability to new technologies.

Nevertheless, early conceptions of *data* as things given or premises are actually critical to moving beyond our present-day obsession with data. As Rosenberg puts it, "For three centuries, the term has served as a kind of historical and epistemological mirror, showing us what we take for granted."[15] In this way, our attitude toward data is a kind of mirror to our society. As Crawford observes, "Data in the twenty-first century became whatever could be captured."[16] And as I posit throughout this book, our obsession with owning, controlling, harvesting, and exploiting it demonstrates the dominant capitalist, instrumentarian impulse that has overtaken the way we value what matters or what counts in our society. This impulse is undermining our attempts at technology governance through data-focused laws and conversations.

Data and the Law

Despite the popularity and ubiquity of *data* in the modern era, neither civil nor common law traditions define what it is. Still, myriad laws and regulations seeking to regulate data use the term in other material definitions and classifications, typically in circular or self-referential ways, treating data as a rhetorical concept or given, in the original spirit of its modern usage. For example, data protection and privacy laws generally define key terms such as *personal data* or *personal information, sensitive data,* or *deidentified data* without actually defining *data* or *information*. Nonetheless, the quickly changing definitions and parameters of these key terms speak volumes about the nature of data as the basis for governing our relationship to digital technologies now and in the future.

The law typically defines *personal data* by reference to things that render, or may render, natural persons identified or identifiable. As early as 1977, Germany's first federal data protection law defined *personal data* as "details on the personal or material circumstances of an identified or identifiable physical person."[17] Modern European data protection law similarly equates *personal data* with "any information relating to an identified or identifiable natural person."[18] And the first comprehensive data protection law enacted in the United States defines *personal information* as "information that identifies, relates to, describes, is capable of being associated with, or could reasonably be linked, directly or indirectly, with a particular consumer or household."[19]

Naturally, the scope of what does or could identify or describe people expands over time as technological capabilities evolve. For instance, in 1995, Europe's first modern data protection law gave just a handful of illustrative examples of what might constitute personal data, including identification numbers and information related to a person's physical, physiological, mental, economic, cultural, or social identity.[20] Reflecting the rise of big data and more advanced data analytics tools as well as the increasing complexity of the digital ecosystem at the time of its enactment, Europe's more recent regulation expands this nonexhaustive list to also include names, location data, online identifiers, and genetic identity information, which were not necessarily foreseen or foreseeable in 1995.[21]

European data protection law also attempts to draw a dubious line between *personal* and *non-personal data*, including through separate regulations pertaining to each. Europe's regulation on *non-personal data*, circularly defined as "any data other than personal data," aims to reduce obstacles to its free flow across borders within the European Union.[22] The recitals to the regulation explain that "the expanding Internet of Things, artificial intelligence and machine learning, represent major sources of non-personal data," and cite "aggregate and anonymized datasets used for big data analytics, data on precision farming that can help to monitor and optimise the use of pesticides and water, or data on maintenance needs for industrial machines," as specific examples of non-personal data. They concede, however, that "if technological developments make it possible to turn anonymised data into personal data, such data are to be treated as personal data," recognizing the instability of these classifications over time and across contexts.[23]

Finally, a similar evolution has occurred around the notion of *sensitive data*. Whereas early national data protection laws did not distinguish between sensitive or special categories of personal data and ordinary personal data, modern frameworks attempt to differentiate them. For example, in 1995, European data protection law identified personal data revealing racial or ethnic origin, political opinions, religious or philosophical beliefs, and trade union membership as well as data concerning health or sex life as *special categories of data* requiring additional protections.[24] Its more recent regulation expands these categories to include genetic data, biometric data, and data concerning a natural person's sexual orientation.[25] State laws in the United States also deem an individual's precise geolocation data, the contents of personal communications, biometric information processed for certain purposes, and limited health-related information as *sensitive personal information*.[26] Entities are typically subject to additional responsibilities and increased liability with respect to their handling of sensitive or special categories of data.

The evolving definitions of terms such as *personal* or *sensitive data* demonstrate the unsettled and ever-expanding nature of these foundational legal concepts. Even as they purport to be "technology neutral," data-centric laws make us increasingly vulnerable over time. As technology evolves to connect more things to the digital pulse of the internet, we inevitably become more identifiable and more exposed, whether or not we are ultimately identified. As a result, what was not previously *personal* or *sensitive data* might become deeply personal or highly sensitive. Moreover, the sensitivity of any given data point depends on the parties with access to it, the economic, social, cultural, and historical context in which it is known, and a variety of other factors. All data points are dynamic and contextual, and cannot be assessed in isolation or stripped of their context. The futility and fragility of these definitions have led several prominent information scholars to reject such categorizations and dichotomies outright, even as many laws continue to rely on them.[27]

Why We Must Go beyond Data

Without question, the notion of data will continue to evolve and evade our best efforts to sufficiently define it. While we cannot realistically govern something we cannot define, focusing on something as abstract and amorphous as data is arguably easier than talking about power, inequality, exploitation, democracy, racism, and misogyny, among other mounting challenges raised by the ongoing evolution of digital technologies. Data has an air of neutrality that veils the deep structural biases and inequities that give rise to our perceived data governance-related challenges. It can act as a kind of distancing tool too, sitting between those who might gain from addressing the root causes of these challenges and those who might lose from disrupting the status quo by questioning the legitimacy of unchecked corporate power, precarious labor practices, environmental impacts, increasing exclusion, and enclosure of the public sphere.

When we start from the perspective of data, we end up with a poverty of framing about the issues at hand and an inability to see beyond data to appreciate what is really at stake. We seek answers to the wrong questions and spin our wheels addressing the wrong problems, sabotaging our efforts at effective harm reduction or risk mitigation strategies along the way. For example, we obsess over *data protection* or *data security*, when we urgently need new frameworks that elevate the protection and safety of *people* above these types of concerns about data. It is why, despite an array of new "privacy"-related legislative proposals, which largely focus on data, we are unlikely to end up better off as individuals or a society.

Moreover, data does not provide a suitable foundation for establishing norms about the way we wish to interact with one another in a technologically mediated world, whether now or in the future. Norms must be grounded in something we can delimit and reach relative consensus about, the way we have in the past with respect to fundamental human rights such as privacy. Without consensus, we risk geopolitical fracturing in the face of collective, cross-border challenges posed by borderless technologies. We can already see this playing out as countries focus on data localization, data nationalism, and data sovereignty, which are really just proxies for other forms of localization, nationalism, and sovereignty more generally.

In part I of this book, I outline the historical origins of our modern approach to data governance, beginning even before digital technologies entered the equation, from its origins in the fundamental human right to privacy through the formation of an early international consensus around the norms for data protection with respect to computerized databases. My approach here, based on my expertise and research, is cross-border, but primarily focused on a transatlantic dialogue about data governance.

In part II, I examine how a more recent shift in the zeitgeist has led lawmakers and policymakers, technologists, industry, and the general public alike to develop a singular obsession with data. As a result, existing legal frameworks often support a narrow, impoverished, and data-centric view of "privacy," or attempt to leverage such a view to protect harms that exceed the scope of what privacy can meaningfully protect. In this way, our obsession with data risks transforming the once-powerful notion of privacy, including as conceptualized in part by data protection laws, into the handmaiden of corporate surveillance and control.

And in the third and final part of this book, I argue that we can avoid this fate by acknowledging the true nature of the brave new postdigital world that is emerging and going beyond our obsession with data to protect people through a more expansive human rights–based approach to technology governance.

My aim in writing this book is to persuade you that we must go beyond data to protect people. If we don't, our data may well end up with more rights and protections than we do.

I

Before Data

1
The Main Frame

For more than fifty years, we have been so busy protecting data that we have largely forgotten to protect people. Roughly since the 1970s, the main frame we have chosen in thinking about data governance is one of *data protection* or *data privacy*. As this would suggest, it is foremost about protecting data and closely linked to a data security mindset. The result is a logic dominated by binary thinking, false dichotomies, hyperindividualism, and an overly narrow view of the digital universe as made up of packets of data somewhere "over there," in line with the nature of 1970s-style databases. This view has been consistently reinforced and exacerbated by the commercial exploitation of the web and digital ecosystem from the 1990s onward.

To understand the story of data governance and how we ended up here, it is important to examine the historical and conceptual origins of the crisis, particularly the context in which our notions of privacy and data protection developed in relation to computing. Through this exploration, it is easier to see how the essence of what we perceive to be a present-day data governance crisis can actually be traced to the evolution of computerized data processing and record keeping in the latter half of the twentieth century as well as the cyberlibertarian ethos of the early web.

Together, they would frame the way we think about data and the governance of digital technologies for decades to come. This "main frame" for thinking about data in the context of databases and the lawlessness of cyberspace has not only profoundly shaped the history of data governance but also has equally profound implications for its future. As we will see, breaking free of this main frame will be critical to moving past the impasse we face and enabling us to imagine a future beyond data.

The Philosophical and Legal Origins of Privacy

When we think of privacy today, we often think of high tech and data-hungry technologies, high-profile data breaches and cyber hacks, *smart* but invasive digital gadgets, and the like. And yet the modern conversation about data and privacy reflects concerns that are much older than data in the digital form of bits and bytes, including more fundamental concerns about privacy, the inviolability of personhood, and autonomy. Privacy itself is a much older concept, and one that long predates computing and the digital age.

References to privacy and the need for a private life can be found in traditional religious texts, ancient Chinese history, and classical Greek philosophy, among other sources. For example, in *Politics*, Aristotle explained that privacy is a moral, philosophical, and political good that allows the individual to cultivate the virtues necessary for healthy participation in public life.[1] Echoes of this kind of separation of public and private life as two distinct spheres would reemerge in early political and legal notions of privacy as a domain free from interference by the state.

As a legal concept, rights related to privacy can be found in several of the world's oldest constitutions—some that are centuries older than computing—even where not expressly characterized as such. Although there is no explicit right to privacy in the US Constitution as ratified by the first Congress in 1791, the Supreme Court has found a general right to privacy to exist in the "penumbrae" created by specific guarantees of several amendments in the Bill of Rights, including the First, Third, Fourth, and Ninth Amendments.[2] For example, the Fourth Amendment, which provides for "the right of the people to be secure in their persons, houses, papers, and effects, against unreasonable searches and seizures," is a constituent component of this right.

Inspired in part by the US Constitution, other early constitutions included similar rights, typically related to the inviolability of a person's home or domicile as well as correspondence or communications. For instance, Norway's constitution, the second-oldest written constitution in the world, adopted in 1814, included an explicit acknowledgment of what we deem to be modern-day human rights, while most other European constitutions at the time contained no express individual rights.[3] In the spirit of the Fourth Amendment to the US Constitution, it stipulated that "domiciliary visits may not be made, except in criminal cases," again protecting the sanctity of one's home or domicile.[4]

Other countries around the world would quickly follow suit. Belgium's constitution, for example, adopted in 1831, proclaimed that "the home is inviolable. No search shall be made except in cases provided for by law and in the form which it prescribes," and also provided that "the secrecy of the mails shall be inviolable."[5] In 1853, Argentina's constitution, which included a bill of rights, likewise declared a right to "the inviolability of the domicile, person, and mail."[6] And in 1919, Finland adopted its first constitution, declaring that "the home peace of Finnish citizens is inviolable," and interestingly, "letter, telegraph, and telephone secrecy is inviolable, unless an exception is provided by law."[7] The specific enumeration of new and emerging modes of communication foreshadowed attempts to leverage traditional constitutional notions of privacy with respect to later digital technologies.

Today, the constitutions of most countries around the world include rights concerned with this kind of inviolability of one's home or domicile, physical person, and papers or communications. In this way, privacy laws imagine a kind of *sphere* or *zone* of privacy—a near physical boundary around the individual, which neither the state nor collective has a right to penetrate, save in exceptional and enumerated circumstances. In fact, the German Constitutional Court has defined it as an "untouchable sphere of private life withdrawn from the influence of state power," echoing the Aristotelian conception of privacy.[8] The notion of *data protection* and mentions of *data* as such in legislation would not emerge until decades later with the digitization of information in the computing age.

International Human Rights Law and Privacy as Protection from Interference by the State

Beginning in the twentieth century, spurred by the industrial age, liberal governments spawned and expanded complex administrative states to accompany their more traditional executive, legislative, and judicial bodies, creating elaborate systems of public records as a by-product.[9] Attempts to catalog and organize citizens and constituents into detailed systems of records were deemed necessary to administer new governmental services and functions. For example, when Congress passed President Franklin Delano Roosevelt's Social Security Act in January 1937, the government suddenly had to keep track of contributions from twenty-six million US citizens and more than three million employers. The newly formed US Social Security Board awarded a contract to the International Business Machines Corporation (IBM), which had specially developed gray punch

IBM Type 77 Collator. *Source:* Wikimedia (https://commons.wikimedia.org/wiki/File :Ibm_type_77.JPG). The Type 77 Collator is licensed under CC BY-SA 3.0 (https:// creativecommons.org/licenses/by-sa/3.0/deed.en).

card–reading machines known as "Type 77 Collators," to help implement and manage its colossal bookkeeping project.[10] And the United States was not alone.

Germany, considered to be the world's first welfare state having introduced healthcare, workers' compensation and injury insurance, and pension funds in the late nineteenth century, also experienced profound changes in the state's relationship to information technologies during the twentieth century.[11] From the formation of the Federal Republic of Germany in 1914 to the post–world wars era, "the German state was engaged in a vast legibility project to map its interior terrain and the lives of its population."[12] Through a combination of population registration and enumeration systems, analog and eventually machine-readable identification cards and other identification documents (including passports), censuses and other population surveys, and other tools, the federal government was gradually able to establish a comprehensive and increasingly integrated information, identification, and control system for its population, administered by the growing bureaucratic state.[13] It was a system that would only become more efficient with the introduction of early computers and computational machines during World War II.

During the world wars, population censuses, national registration systems, and conscription systems for military service became commonplace in much of the Western world.[14] As they got more sophisticated, these databases and systems of record keeping would play an increasing role in aiding governments to commit wartime atrocities too (and eventually, peacetime surveillance).[15] In World War I, punch cards and early information technologies were developed to administer the conscription of members into the military. In its aftermath, these same tools were leveraged for other purposes, and additional surveillance tools and technologies were developed as a response to the fraught international political climate and crises, paving the way for their use in the next world war.[16] As one archivist has mused, the initial defeat of the French in World War II was due to the fact that the Germans "had entered the war with a better filing system."[17]

The trauma of two sequential world wars, and in particular the Nazis' racially motivated atrocities in the Second World War, helped "cement international consensus in the form of the United Nations as a bulwark against war and for the preservation of peace," and would shape the values that informed modern-day notions of privacy.[18] In 1948, in the fog of war, the UN General Assembly adopted the Universal Declaration of Human Rights (UDHR), which declared the right to privacy as a fundamental human right.[19]

As with national frameworks before it, international human rights law conceived of privacy as delimiting the boundaries of one's family, home, and correspondence in relation to interferences by the state. Only now it included an explicit reference to *privacy* itself.[20] Article 12 of the declaration proclaimed, "No one shall be subject to arbitrary interference with his *privacy*, family, home or correspondence," and that the state has an obligation to provide protection from the law against such interferences. It would later be codified as a fundamental right of the individual under international human rights law in Article 17 of the International Covenant on Civil and Political Rights (ICCPR) in 1966 as a right to affirmative protections of the law against "arbitrary or unlawful interference or attacks."[21] Though fundamental, the human right to privacy is not absolute and can be interfered with where prescribed by law, and necessary and proportionate to achieve a legitimate aim, such as for the purposes of national security.[22]

Advances in computing and networked technologies in the second half of the twentieth century would challenge these traditional notions of privacy as a kind of bounded protection from interference by the state of the individual's person, home, effects, and even correspondence, which before electronic or digital communications, still required a physical interference or intrusion.

Advances in Computing Challenge Traditional Notions of Privacy

In the aftermath of World War II, wartime research and development boosted industry, driving rapid technological advancement and increasing the volume of transactions requiring records about people. Following the introduction of the Electronic Numerator Integrator and Computer (ENIAC), the world's first general-purpose electronic computer in 1946, advances in computing would radically transform the way that public records were collected, disseminated, and used. ENIAC's creators would also go on to develop an original computer designed for use by the US Census Bureau, the Universal Automatic Computer (UNIVAC), which would become the first major civilian computer and bring the census into the computing age.[23] In the 1950s, the UNIVAC was used to tabulate the census and undertake a series of economic surveys, among its other uses.

Again, the United States was not alone. In the 1960s, the German government began investing in information technology as well as electronic data processing research and development programs. In 1967, it launched its first in a series of programs designed to promote computer applications, education, and research and development. In 1971, it renewed the program with more than six times the original budget to develop computers, peripherals, software, applications, and components as well as fund relevant academic research.[24] By the early 1970s, tensions emerged between various committees within the German Bundestag with conflicting views on the risks and benefits posed by computers and data processing capabilities. While the interior department was enamored with efficiencies in information gathering, the legal committee was concerned about the risks to individuals of putting efficient record keeping above their personal interests in privacy and related rights—a tension echoed in present-day debates.[25]

Two women reprogramming the ENIAC computer. *Source:* ARL Technical Library (https://commons.wikimedia.org/wiki/File:Reprogramming_ENIAC.png).

Later in the twentieth century, as computers went from exclusively military-grade equipment to commercially available hardware, Western governments, which were early to the computing age, began keeping digital records and creating databases of information about their constituents. "By the 1960s, attractive prices, persuasive salesmen, and ingenious computer software services had stimulated the introduction of automated data processing equipment into a great many record-keeping organizations."[26] This rapid computerization enabled the collection, storage, and processing of vast amounts of data, creation of large databases, and use of data in new forms of decision-making about the subjects of that data, both as individuals and at the population level, across different facets of life, including decisions about credit, insurance, and housing as well as access to benefits and services. This uptick in computerized record keeping and data processing by governments in the 1960s raised considerable public concern about privacy, as would the birth of the internet at the end of the decade.[27]

The internet we know today was born out of a technical research project sponsored by the US Department of Defense's Advanced Research Projects Agency (ARPA, renamed DARPA in 1972), which created a small network for connecting computers remotely known as ARPANET. The network, which initially consisted of four computers at the University of California at Los Angeles, Stanford Research Institute, University of California at Santa Barbara, and University of Utah, was designed for *packet-switching*—a method of disassembling a message into small segments or *packets* of data that could be more easily transmitted through a network, and then reassembling these pieces on arrival at the intended destination. ARPANET made its first successful transmission of a packet-switched message between the University of California at Los Angeles and Stanford Research Institute on October 29, 1969.[28] Though sponsored by the military, the original aim of the network was to enable academic and scientific research centers to share computing resources.[29]

For more than a decade, ARPANET would remain a small, single network operated by a collegial core of engineers and scientists who were well-known to each other, gradually connecting to additional universities and research centers.[30] As the early internet pioneers knew each other and were part of a relatively small network of networks with limited applications, designing and building an identity layer into the internet's architecture as well as concerns about individual privacy were not priorities. Rather, the network was conceived of as connecting computers or machines, not people, just as early internet protocols were designed to identify network resources, not people.[31] For these technicians, *privacy* was synonymous with *anonymity*; like code, this was a kind of binary condition of either being known or unknown to a network, not a complicated sociotechnical concept that exists on a nonbinary spectrum.

And with a clear separation between the analog world and digital domain of computing, it was easy to think of data as mere packets of information transmitted via information and communications technology (ICT)—as something *over there* in a database.

But all of that changed in 1983 when ARPANET adopted a new communications protocol that would enable the exchange of data packets between different and distant networks, resulting in a network of networks we would come to know as the *internet*.[32] Computers and networked technologies like the internet penetrated the physical boundaries of our private sphere, providing governments with access to information about us, and challenging our traditional notions of privacy in relation to our bodies, homes, and even correspondence. Unlike correspondence in the possession of its sender or recipient, records and databases were controlled by the government, and not in one's possession or control. And unlike physical papers and effects, data could live in different places at the same time, meaning that an intrusion or interference need not be physical. At the same time, governments had an interest in the use of this data for supplying new services to their constituents. Data protection was born from this tension between the individual's right to privacy and collective interests of society vis-à-vis governments.

Early Data Protection Laws Emerge in Response to Government Databases

The same advances in computing that allowed governments to harness new data processing capabilities and computerized databases also prompted the need to define the rights of individuals over the information contained in those databases. It was in this context of computerized, state-operated databases that the first national *data protection laws* were introduced in the 1970s and early 1980s. This is when the fundamental right to privacy, originally conceived of in the context of constitutional and human rights law, took an *ICT turn* in the form of data protection. It is arguably when an obsession with data as a problem to solve took hold too.

Motivated by mounting concerns over the government's ability to leverage official databases, and enhanced computing abilities to make decisions about individuals and their affairs, early data protection laws can be understood as a kind of secondary right deriving from more traditional notions of privacy. Data protection was designed to cover situations where individuals were known (originally, to the state) by way of their relationships or roles as citizens or constituents. It imposed certain responsibilities and obligations on those with authorized access to personal data, and viewed unauthorized access, such as sharing this data without someone's knowledge or consent, as a kind of violation of the individual's fundamental right to privacy. In the US context, the term *privacy* or *data privacy* is often used to refer to this derivative right of *data protection*.[33]

Early data protection laws were largely limited in scope, and were primarily, but not exclusively, concerned with official records and databases—typically those maintained by government entities. They were largely focused on the activities and responsibilities of database owners and operators, holding them accountable for the accuracy, integrity, and security of data, and frequently created new administrative bodies to oversee the licensing and registration of such databases. To the extent that they introduced new individual rights, such rights were usually limited to the rights to access and rectify data maintained in those databases, similar to the writ of *habeas data* (Latin for "we command you have the data") that would later emerge in Latin American countries, as further described below.

Perhaps unsurprisingly, the first modern data protection law emerged in West Germany in response to the establishment of new public data processing facilities and computerized databases.

Motivated in part by the trauma of East Germany's secret police, the Stasi, which would screen, search, and catalog the contents of people's homes and correspondence, the West German state of Hesse enacted the Hessische Datenschutzgesetz (Hesse Data Protection Act) in 1970. The act only applied to the public sector, regulating files containing the personal information of citizens that were stored by the local government, including the automatic processing, storage, and use of that information. It also contained confidentiality requirements to regulate the conduct of personnel with access to the computers and personal records and introduced the modern notion of *datensicheriung* or *data security*.[34]

Notably, the Hesse Data Protection Act was the first legal instrument to use the German word *daten* (or *data*), instead of a more generic word like *information*, as a term of art that specifically referred to data in digital form or processed by computers. Hesse was soon followed by Rhineland-Palatinate and other German federal states, which would also embrace the notion and use the term *data protection*.[35] Shortly thereafter, the first national laws related to data protection were enacted elsewhere in Europe.

Sweden, which became one of the earliest and most computerized societies in the world, was the first country to enact a national data protection law in 1973.[36] The Swedish Datalag or Data Act covered the processing of personal data in computerized registers or databases, and required each database operator to obtain a license from the newly created Data Inspection Board prior to such processing.[37] Although Sweden's law applied to all computerized databases or *registers*, whether maintained by the government or otherwise, the law was born out of an intense public debate over the 1970 Census of Population and Housing, which focused on the increasing availability and access to personal data by official authorities as well as the insufficiency of existing laws to address the associated risks. Nevertheless, the generality and broad scope of the law made it theoretically adaptable to the commercially owned and operated databases that quickly proliferated in the immediate after-math of its enactment. In practice, however, it would quickly prove ill-equipped and unfit for the purpose of regulating private sector uses of data.[38]

Germany soon followed suit, passing its first federal data protection law in 1977. Known as the Bundesdatenschutzgesetz (BDSG), the law aimed to prohibit "the misuse of personal data . . . and thereby to prevent harm to any personal interests that warrants protection." It was designed as a blanket prohibition on all processing of personal data except where expressly authorized by law or where the data subject has given their prior written consent to the processing. Like the Swedish law before it, the BDSG established a new federal authority, the Federal Commissioner for Data Protection, to help oversee the law's application in the public sector. While the BDSG applied to the processing of personal data by the private sector, the law set out distinct rules along with a separate supervisory and enforcement framework for those private sector rules. It also distinguished between internal and commercial uses of personal data by the private sector, with considerably less protection for individuals from the commercial use and exploitation of their data by companies.[39]

In 1978, France enacted Law 78–17 on Information Technologies, Data Files, and Civil Liberties, boldly declaring in Article 1 that "information technology should be at the service of every citizen [and] shall not violate human identity, human rights, privacy, or individual or public liberties." Like the Swedish law, France's law required the government to register public databases—in this case, with the Commission national d'informatique et des liberté—stating the purpose of the database, nature of the personal data collected, and sources of and destinations for that data. It also recognized the individual's right to access their information, request the correction or completion of incorrect or incomplete information, and exercise some control over the distribution of that information.[40] Similar national data protection laws soon followed in Germany, Spain, the United Kingdom, and Netherlands.[41]

Here it is worth noting a slightly different approach taken in Latin America, where computing at scale was slower to emerge than in the United States and Europe. Once it did, the same concerns arose with respect to databases. Latin America, however, had a slightly different attitude toward the subject based on its unique cultural, historical, and political circumstances, particularly with respect to fresh government abuses of records and databases. In the 1990s, several Latin American countries, emerging from political turmoil and extensive human rights abuses suffered under dictatorships, codified a writ of habeas data in their constitutions.

In 1988, Brazil would become the first Latin American country to include a writ of habeas data in its constitution, soon to be followed by Columbia in 1991, Paraguay in 1992, Peru in 1993, Argentina in 1994, Bolivia in 1995, Ecuador in 1996, and Venezuela in 1999.[42] Originally created to help families in search of loved ones who went missing as a result of forced disappearances and extrajudicial executions at the hands of dictators (known as *desaparecidos*), the constitutional writ of habeas data was broadly designed to protect citizens from the improper collection and use of personal data by authorities. The writ of habeas data afforded citizens the right to petition their government for access to personal information collected and held about them as well as the opportunity to challenge or correct that data. In this way, it was similar in spirit to early data protection laws that emerged in other parts of the world.

An International Consensus Emerges around Fair Information Practice Principles

Perhaps ironically, given the state of privacy laws in the United States today, one of the earliest and most ambitious frameworks actually emerged there in the 1970s. As in Europe, the rise of computerized databases and digital record keeping within US government agencies resulted in mounting concerns about the technological and legal issues raised by these systems, culminating in the appointment of the Advisory Committee on Automated Personal Data Systems within the Department of Health, Education, and Welfare (HEW). In 1973, after a comprehensive investigation that also examined the Hessian and Swedish data protection laws then in force, the HEW committee published its findings in a report titled *Records, Computers, and the Rights of Citizens*.

Prefaced as a "report about changes in American society which may result from using computers to keep records about people," it highlighted growing tensions between the efficiency of record keeping and data processing tools and the individual's right to privacy. The report also expressed concerns about "putting record-keeping in the hands of a new class of data-processing specialists" and the risks of treating "questions of record-keeping practice which involve issues of social policy . . . as if they were nothing more than questions of efficient technique."[43] In the context of the current state of affairs with respect to data governance, these were prescient questions at the time.

Critically, the HEW Report outlined a federal code of Fair Information Practices (FIPs) for all automated personal data systems. The code consisted of five core principles (which did not include the notion of "consent"):

- There must be no personal data record-keeping systems whose very existence is secret.
- There must be a way for an individual to find out what information about him is in a record and how it is used.
- There must be a way for an individual to prevent information about him that was obtained for one purpose from being used or made available for other purposes without his consent.
- There must be a way for an individual to correct or amend a record of identifiable information about him.

- Any organization creating, maintaining, using, or disseminating records of identifiable personal data must assure the reliability of the data for their intended use and must take precautions to prevent misuse of the data.[44]

Drawing on the HEW's FIPs, the US Congress passed the Privacy Act of 1974 in an attempt to regulate the collection, maintenance, use, and dissemination of personal information by federal executive branch agencies.[45]

Prompted by the Watergate scandal and mounting concerns about the surveillance of individuals by the government, the Privacy Act sought to balance the government's interest in maintaining records about individuals with the individual's privacy interests vis-à-vis their personal information. The act, which applied to records that could identify an individual (but not aggregate or anonymized records), prohibited covered agencies from disclosing records about an individual without the prior written consent of the subject of that record (albeit with twelve broad exceptions), established penalties for unauthorized disclosures, and provided the individual with limited rights to access and amend such records.[46] The FIPs, as codified by the Privacy Act, became foundational to numerous other national and international principles as well as legal frameworks in the decades to come. The original FIPs and subsequent principles inspired by them would together come to be known as the Fair Information Practice Principles (FIPPs). In the early 1980s, international organizations, including the Organisation for Economic Co-operation and Development (OECD) and the Council of Europe, also sought to address the impacts of automated data processing.

In 1980, the OECD adopted the Guidelines on the Protection of Privacy and Transborder Flows of Personal Data (the OECD Guidelines). The OECD Guidelines, the first internationally agreed-on set of data protection principles, aimed to strike a balance between the protection of the individual's rights in relation to personal data and the commercial interests in the free flow of information across borders. Their adoption was motivated, in large part, over concerns about inconsistent and competing national data protection laws enacted in response to new and automated means of processing data.[47] The guidelines set out seven core principles largely mirroring the FIPPs—transparency, individual control, use limitation, purpose limitation, data minimization, data integrity, and security—and importantly, introduced a new, eighth core principle of accountability.

The first legally binding international instrument to extend to both the public and private sectors took a similar approach. In 1981, the Council of Europe concluded the Convention for the Protection of Individuals with Regard to Automatic Processing of Personal Data. Known as Convention 108, it was the first legally binding international instrument to expressly recognize a right to *data protection* in relation to automated personal data files and the automatic processing of personal data.[48] Its preamble expressed the council's desire to "extend the safeguards for everyone's rights and fundamental freedoms, and in particular the right to the respect for privacy, taking account of the increasing flow across frontiers of personal data undergoing *automatic processing*." As it was largely built on the FIPPs, Convention 108 would also lay the groundwork for transposing this public sector–inspired framework to the private sector.[49]

That the FIPPs would form the core of national laws on both sides of the Atlantic, and inspire the first international set of guiding principles and regional frameworks, including the Asia-Pacific Economic Cooperation's privacy regime, demonstrates the broad international consensus that had formed around them by the 1980s.[50] Despite many variations on these principles, the FIPPs boiled down to four broad categories of principles derived from the original FIPs—notice/awareness, access/participation, choice/consent, and integrity/security—plus a fifth core principle related to enforcement or redress, as later summarized by the US Federal Trade

Commission.[51] Although some local or regional frameworks had additional principles, they typically featured variations on these core themes.

While international consensus crystallized around this 1970s' main frame, as ultimately captured in the FIPPs in the 1980s, technological advances in commercial and household computing as well as the commercialization of the internet would far exceed the scope envisioned by the national and international legal frameworks then in existence. In turn, early data protection laws conceived of before such advances, in the narrow context of ICT databases, would prove woefully inadequate, particularly as they emphasized *data* as an organizing principle.

Unfortunately, this decades-old logic, encoded in our early approaches to data protection, still persists in large measure today, even as it is no longer fit for purpose. Instead, it is hampering the way we interpret and apply existing data-related laws and regulations, while also diminishing the urgency of designing better ones to reflect the substantially different technological realities (and relationships to technology) that we face. Worse yet, it is fundamentally failing to protect people.

2

Update Failed

Visions are colliding between, firstly, states like China [which] argue that the government determines the limits of freedom and ultimately owns data generated by digital technology; secondly, the United States, where, in the name of free markets, data is another locus for competition between companies and consumers: and thirdly Europe, where according to the European Convention on Human Rights and the Charter of Fundamental Rights of the EU, data doesn't belong to anyone but privacy is something inalienable and personal data is something to be treated with respect.
—former European data protection supervisor Giovanni Butarelli

In January 2022, the world was stunned when the island nation of Tonga was cut off from all internet communications after a volcanic eruption and the ensuing tsunami damaged the underwater internet cables that connect it to the rest of the world. Apart from incidents like these, it can be easy to forget that vast networks of physical submarine cables, consisting of silica glass optical fibers coated in plastic, copper, and steel, are essential for the delivery of an array of cable, internet, and other modern telecommunications services to billions of people around the world. Digital technologies do not just connect us virtually; they quite literally connect us.

And yet while our laws are jurisdictional, predominantly local and national in reach, digital and data-driven technologies do not respect borders. In fact, the technological disregard for borders is only growing starker with the proliferation of new decentralized and networked technologies, such as blockchain or distributed ledger technologies and cryptocurrencies. As such, we should not underestimate the importance of international consensus around the standards and norms that should govern the use of such borderless digital technologies through otherwise jurisdictionally limited law and policy frameworks.

As outlined in chapter 1, common principles for data protection, particularly with respect to information maintained in government databases, first emerged in the 1970s as the FIPs in the United States and early national data protection laws across Europe. In turn, they would help foster broad international consensus in the form of the OECD's nonbinding Guiding Principles and Council of Europe's binding Convention 108 around FIPPs in the 1980s. But almost as quickly as this consensus formed, approaches to data governance would begin to diverge across the Atlantic as a result of the unique political and economic circumstances of each geography. While the United States would pursue a combination of limited, sector-specific privacy laws coupled with a market-based, self-regulatory approach, Europe would embrace a comprehensive, human rights-based framework.[1]

This chapter explores how international consensus around data protection unraveled in the face of rapid technological evolution and a burgeoning data-driven digital economy, eventually undermining efforts to upgrade our legal frameworks and losing sight of the original aims of data protection, resulting in the heightened geopolitical fracturing around technology governance we encounter today.

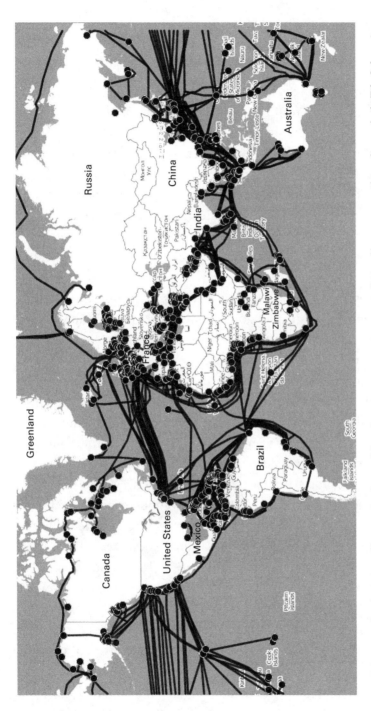

World map of submarine communication cables. *Source:* openstreetmap.org (https://commons.wikimedia.org/wiki/File:Submarine _cable_map_umap.png). "World Map of Submarine Communication Cables" is licensed under CC BY-SA 3.0 (https://creativecommons .org/licenses/by-sa/3.0/deed.en).

As International Consensus around Data Protection Emerges, so Does a New Digital Economy

At the time when consensus was forming around the FIPPs, most data in the digital realm lived in a relational, presumptively legitimate context of a one-to-one relationship between the government and an individual citizen or constituent. Much later on in the evolution of the digital landscape, it would extend to a one-to-one relationship between private companies and their individual customers or consumers. In both cases, the individual citizen or consumer was known and not anonymous in this relationship, identified by their legal or commercial relationship to a known entity. Before the rise of big data and sophisticated analytics, the database was a mere digital representation of its analog predecessor and presented largely the same risks, apart from additional concerns about data security, storage, and protection from hacking. Moreover, given the limited scope of the *online* or digital world at the time, perceived threats to privacy were of limited concern. But this would change significantly with the growth of household and commercial computing along with the emergence of the World Wide Web (the *web*) in 1989. In particular, the web, built on top of the internet's networking infrastructure, would transition us from the database age into the information age without the laws to match.

Commercial and household uses of computers burgeoned in the 1970s, beginning with the release of the first commercially produced microprocessor and first personal computer (PC) in 1971. By 1977, which saw the release of the Apple II, Commodore PET, and TRS-80—commonly known as the 1977 Trinity—PCs would become relatively affordable and accessible to households, ushering in the *PC revolution*.[2] In the 1980s, PCs were rapidly and widely adopted by companies for business use too. Interestingly, countries that were early adopters of national data protection laws in the 1970s and 1980s were also early adopters of household and workplace computers, and experienced exponential rates of uptake. For example, the penetration of computers in the United States rapidly increased from less than 5 percent of the population in 1981 to more than one-third of the population by 1995.[3] Similarly, the number of households with computers in the United Kingdom more than doubled in the same time period.[4] Computers also penetrated home life in Sweden quickly, with computers for personal or professional use found in 51 percent of Swedish households by 1995, more than double the number of households with them in 1984.[5]

Alongside the PC revolution, a number of important, successive technological innovations in the 1980s would transition the internet from its largely academic and research-oriented foundations into a vast commercial opportunity.[6] Between 1981 and 1983, Ethernet products would enable resource sharing between computers in *local area networks* (LANs), making it easier to bring additional PCs online and drastically enlarging the internet as a result.[7] A year later, Telenet became the internet's first commercial network, broadening access to the internet and allowing for *electronic mail* (or *email*) to be sent across borders. In 1983, ARPANET adopted a new communications protocol known as the *Transmission Control Protocol / Internet Protocol* (TCP/IP), which enabled the exchange of data packets between different and distant networks. While TCP would continue to enable *packet switching*, IP provided the addressing and forwarding information necessary to locate as well as route those messages between the correct machines connected to the network, creating a network of networks that would come to be known as the internet.

The same year, the *Domain Name System* (DNS) was created to manage the increasing number of users on the internet, making it easier to navigate and thereby also boosting its popularity. In just a few years following the invention of DNS, the number of hosts on the network grew by more than fifteen times.[8] And yet while more and more people were exchanging emails, reading news, and sharing files online, some specialized knowledge of computing was still necessary to access and use the internet effectively, in large part due to a lack of standardization in the way that documents were structured and formatted online.

That standardization arrived in 1989 when a research fellow named Tim Berners-Lee and his colleagues at the European Organization for Nuclear Research developed the *hypertext markup language* (HTML) and *uniform resource locator* (URL) as a way of structuring and linking all the information available on a computer network to make it quickly as well as easily accessible.[9] Although originally conceived of and developed to meet the demand for automated information sharing between scientists in universities and research institutes around the world, Berners-Lee's standardization would eventually connect with TCP/IP and DNS, giving birth to the web, and making it easier for ordinary users to publish and access information online.

The web, coupled with the launch of web browsers, beginning with the Mosaic browser in 1993, allowed people to discover and create their own HTML web pages. The internet skyrocketed in popularity seemingly overnight, with the number of websites growing from 130 in 1993 to over 100,000 at the start of 1996.[10] In just one year, 1995, Microsoft introduced Windows 95, early internet pioneers Amazon, Yahoo!, and eBay were born, Internet Explorer was released, and the Java programming language was introduced, allowing for animation on websites while creating a burst of e-commerce and other online activities. By 1995, the internet and web were established phenomena, ushering in the new *digital economy*.[11]

Motivated by Economics, Europe Attempts to Upgrade Its Data Protection Laws

As the digital economy boomed on one side of the Atlantic, a process of political and economic integration was taking place on the other. Twelve European states, aiming to form a single internal market and eventually move toward a common currency in the form of the euro, formalized their political union in the Treaty on the European Union in Maastricht in 1992.[12] As household and commercial computing expanded, the proliferation of national laws and splintering of rules across geographic borders hampered the free flow of information along with the emerging commercial trade facilitated by the internet and web.

By the mid-1990s, it was clear that the commercialization of the internet and web had ushered in a new era of cross-border digital technologies and data flows. And as the European Union grew, it also quickly became apparent that the fragmented approach to privacy and data protection across various member states, including differing levels of individual protections afforded by their early national data protection laws, was creating barriers to free trade and the cross-border flow of data, threatening the completion of the internal market.[13] This would become a core motivation for the first modern data protection laws to cover the private sector as robustly as the public sector.

In 1995, more than two decades after the first national data protection laws emerged in Europe, the Data Protection Directive 95/46/EC of the European Parliament and Council of October 24, 1995, on the protection of individuals with regard to the processing of personal data and the free movement of such data (95/46/EC) (the Directive) would become the first modern data protection law of the digital era. Per the recitals to the Directive, divergent national laws and administrative provisions resulted in "a difference in levels of protection of the rights and freedoms of individuals, notably the right to privacy, with regard to the processing of personal data afforded in the Member States [and constituted] an obstacle to the pursuit of a number of economic activities at Community level."[14] In order to remove these obstacles to flows of personal data, the Directive set out to ensure that the level of protection of the rights and freedoms of individuals with regard to the processing of personal data would be equivalent in all member states.

The Directive was intended to be a comprehensive, rights-based approach to data protection. It was *comprehensive* in the sense of an omnibus law that is broadly applicable to all processing of personal data, across any sector, whether public or private, and *rights-based* in the sense of being grounded in certain fundamental rights of the individual that emanate from European and international human rights law, including the right to privacy per Article 8 of the European Convention for the Protection of Human Rights and Fundamental Freedoms. The Directive was the first clear articulation of a host of individual data subject rights, including the right to be informed about data processing activities, the right to access one's personal data, the right to rectify incomplete or inaccurate data, limited rights to restrict or object to certain processing, a limited right to erasure of certain personal data, and certain rights with respect to automated decision-making. It also introduced some key administrative and supervisory functions as well as new enforcement and redress mechanisms.[15]

In substance, the Directive was heavily inspired by the FIPPs as codified in the OECD Guiding Principles and Convention 108.[16] All three instruments shared the common core principles of legitimacy, data quality or accuracy, purpose limitation, security and confidentiality, notice and transparency, participation or access, and accountability. Although the Directive introduced a series of lawful bases for processing personal data, processing on the basis of the data subject's consent would come to predominate in practice in the context of online services, as further examined below.

While the Directive set out to promote the free flow of information and eliminate barriers to commerce within the European Union, it simultaneously imposed new obstacles outside its borders. Specifically, the Directive prohibited transfers of personal data to third countries without an "adequate level of protection" in place, with limited exceptions.[17] This feature of European data protection law would lead to considerable tensions between Europe and other globally dominant economies, including the United States, particularly in light of the borderless nature of modern digital technologies and resultant data flows.

In July 2000, in an effort to resolve those tensions, the United States and European Union negotiated and approved a *safe harbor* framework developed by the US Department of Commerce.[18] This framework established a set of binding fair data information practices for the participating organizations, subject to enhanced enforcement and oversight by the US Federal Trade Commission and US Department of Transportation. But as the commercial web continued to spawn a series of rapid technological changes and innovations, the sweeping transformation of the digital economy drove a growing wedge into transatlantic relations over data flows and data sharing. This wedge, which would eventually lead to the unraveling and renegotiation of the safe harbor arrangement, also created economic incentives that threatened the original aims of data protection in the spirit of the FIPPs.

US Law and Policymakers Reinterpret the FIPPs to Favor Commerce

As Europe was endeavoring to harmonize its laws around a comprehensive, rights-based framework, the United States was embracing an economic boom, enabled in large part by a policy shift toward an era of deregulation that began with President Ronald Regan and was further cemented by President Bill Clinton. As the internet surged in popularity and US tech companies prospered, the United States entered one of the longest-running bull markets in history, lasting from October 1990 through the turn of the century, during which the US primary stock market index rose by 417 percent.[19] As one researcher notes, "The idea of a new technological age played a key role in the mind of the 1990s' bull market."[20]

Reluctant to stifle present and future innovation and commerce spawned by internet-based technologies in the 1990s, the Clinton administration took a hands-off approach to e-commerce. In a 1997 report titled *A Framework for Global Electronic Commerce*, the administration asserted that "commerce on the Internet could total tens of billions of dollars by the turn of the century" and officially embraced industry self-regulation. Core guiding principles in the report included that "the private sector should lead," "governments should avoid undue restrictions on electronic commerce," and "governments should recognize the unique qualities of the Internet."[21]

A year later, the US Federal Trade Commission all but officially endorsed a paradigm for consumer data privacy that reduced the original breadth and complexity of the FIPPs to just two principles: notice and choice. As legal scholar Fred Cate observes, "At their inception in the 1970s and early 1980s, FIPPS were broad, aspirational, and included a blend of substantive (e.g., data quality, use limitation) and procedural (e.g., consent, access) principles. They reflected a wide consensus about the need for broad standards to facilitate both individual privacy and the promise of information flows in an increasingly technology-dependent, global society." As translated into national law in subsequent decades, however, the FIPPS were increasingly reduced to narrow, legalistic principles, such as notice and choice, reflecting a "procedural approach to maximizing individual control over data rather than individual or societal welfare."[22]

The *notice and choice* paradigm was predicated on the idea that with sufficient information about the purposes and nature of data collection and use, individuals could make informed decisions about, and consent to, that collection and use. In contrast to the omnibus approach of Europe's Data Protection Directive of 1995, the United States would take a sectoral approach to privacy, extending this paradigm through a variety of sector-specific laws and regulations passed in the 1990s, including the Health Insurance Portability and Accountability Act of 1996, Children's Online Privacy Protection Act of 1998, and Gramm-Leach Bliley Act of 1999, which requires certain covered financial institutions to provide consumers with an annual privacy notice.[23]

Reflecting the relatively narrow scope of the digital realm at the time, the approach was at least philosophically cogent. Yet extending an approach that was conceived of in the narrow context of government databases to an ever-expanding digital realm, including as a core consumer protection strategy in commercial settings, would prove fatal to the initially lofty aims for data protection as a derivative right of privacy. As Cate laments, "The greatest failure of FIPPS as applied today is the substitution of maximizing consumer choice for the original goal of protecting privacy while permitting data flows. As a result, the energy of data processors, legislators, and enforcement authorities has been squandered on notices and often meaningless consent opportunities, rather than on enhancing privacy."[24] Through the US approach, the original spirit and aims of data protection as an extension of the fundamental right to privacy dimmed, and international consensus began to fracture.

The US approach was also enabled by the philosophy of the early web and its cyberlibertarian ethos, marked by a kind of binary thinking about separate *online* and *offline* worlds. Early internet pioneers believed they had designed an entirely new realm of existence known as *cyberspace*—a realm that should not be subject to the laws of physics or governments that apply to the *real world*. In 1996, John Perry Barlow, cofounder of the Electronic Frontier Foundation, published his famous (or infamous, depending on one's perspective) cyberlibertarian manifesto, "A Declaration of the Independence of Cyberspace."[25] The manifesto was written in response to the passage of the Communications Decency Act in the US Congress—an early and unusual effort to combat the growing amount of objectionable material online, and the first federal law to attempt to apply any rules at all to the internet (before Clinton's 1997 report set out policy-squashing efforts).[26]

Barlow proclaimed, "I declare the global social space we are building to be naturally independent of the tyrannies you seek to impose on us. You have no moral right to rule us nor do you possess any methods of enforcement we have true reason to fear. . . . Ours is a world that is both everywhere and nowhere, but it is not where bodies live."[27] Barlow's vision was a digital realm separate from the physical or material one. The mythical separation between the real world and cyberspace would continue to undermine efforts to curtail commercial uses of data, or address the related questions of anonymity, identity, and privacy "online." As captured by a now-famous 1993 *New Yorker* cartoon, the adage became, "On the internet, nobody knows you're a dog," reinforcing the notion of the internet as a kind of digital realm, distinct from the physical one. It would also dampen the urgency or perceived need for new laws or regulations, including those related to the original aims of data protection and more fundamental rights to privacy. This ethos still permeates the discourse about internet governance today.[28]

While other digital pioneers espoused competing visions of a more collective, community-based internet, Barlow's cyberlibertarian vision ultimately won out as it "attracted entrepreneurs like Eric Schmidt and Steve Wozniak, who hoped to carve out new markets in a digital world unrestrained by national borders or government regulations."[29] As Google's early CEO, Schmidt, alongside Google cofounders Larry Page and Sergey Brin, would become a chief architect of these new markets. Google would become the first of many companies to claim human experience as free raw materials for the hidden commercial practices of extraction, prediction, and sales, creating a new market for human behavioral futures—a practice and economic logic known as *surveillance capitalism*.[30]

Relying on frictionless flows of this behavioral surplus through new markets, surveillance capitalism would spawn an entire shadow digital economy, consisting of advertising technology inter-mediaries such as ad exchange platforms, data brokers, and myriad unknown third parties that lurk in the shadows of digital interactions and transactions. Once it took hold, the logic of surveillance capitalism would incentivize the datafication of everything, creating a world where "no thing counts until it is rendered as behavior, translated into electronic data flows, and channeled into the light as observable data," as further explored in part III of this book.[31]

Because laws and regulations could impede this free flow and rendering, maintaining lawlessness was critical to the success of surveillance capitalism. To avoid regulation, Schmidt and the other surveillance capitalists argued that the state could never keep pace with technology companies, rendering attempts at regulation futile, and that any regulation would merely stifle unbridled innovation, setting the United States behind its economic rivals. In other words, they leveraged the cyberlibertarian ethos espoused by Barlow to avoid regulations, even as they expended significant resources lobbying lawmakers at home and in other countries.

The surveillance capitalists were also beneficiaries of the tragic events that unfolded on September 11, 2001. Despite increasing motivation and interest from lawmakers in online privacy in the years leading up to 9/11, the terrorist attacks thwarted any momentum for legislative efforts in the United States, instead ushering in an era of surveillance exceptionalism and contributing to the rise of surveillance capitalism. As the US government came to see the internet and large Silicon Valley companies as instrumental to the intelligence community's mission, it pushed for sweeping and extraordinary measures that privileged security over privacy or liberty, including the USA PATRIOT Act, which dramatically increased the government's ability to surveil and collect information about

individuals. Silicon Valley was all too happy to sustain this perception to keep regulations at bay.

Gradually, this combination of deregulation, a persistent cyberlibertarian ethos, and the logic of surveillance capitalism aided
by surveillance exceptionalism would contribute to the rise of
hegemonic technology corporations in the United States, including Google, Apple, Facebook (now Meta), Amazon, and Microsoft
(sometimes referred to as *big tech*). As a result of this economic con-
centration, these US tech titans would come to exert tremendous
influence over foreign and domestic legislatures, obtain market
dominance over much of the world's population, and set the terms
of the debate around data governance for decades to come, all the
while undermining efforts to design effective modern legal frameworks to protect the fundamental rights at issue in early attempts at
data protection.[32]

Europe Endeavors to Modernize Its Data Protection Laws

As the digital economy boomed in the United States, Europe was
still struggling to remove barriers across the Single Market, including with respect to data flows. The Directive had not delivered the
kind of harmonization it was intended to provide with regard to
data protection, in part due to the nature of a directive under European law. Lagging behind the United States and other allies in the
digital economy, as e-commerce and cross-border data flows continued to increase, Europe turned its attention to promoting economic
growth. Following the introduction of the euro in 1999, the European Commission adopted Directive 2000/31/EC of the European
Parliament and Council of June 8, 2000, on certain legal aspects of
information society services, in particular electronic commerce, in
the internal market (the e-Commerce Directive). The e-Commerce
Directive, which applied to businesses and consumers, sought to

harmonize laws for doing business online and limit the liability of commercial actors. Data protection would not be back on the table for more than a decade.

When Regulation (EU) 2016/679 of the European Parliament and Council of April 27, 2016, on the protection of natural persons with regard to the processing of personal data and the free movement of such data, and repealing Directive 95/46/EC (General Data Protection Regulation) (the GDPR) was formally proposed by the European Commission in 2012, the commission argued that the legislation was necessary to achieve greater harmonization of the law across member states in light of profound technological changes since the Directive's adoption and new challenges posed to cross-border commerce in an expanding Single Market.

While the Directive had set out common standards for data protection, it allowed each member state to pursue its own way of achieving them. By the time the GDPR was introduced, the European Union had nearly doubled in size, and those common standards had evolved into more than two dozen divergent national laws. As a regulation rather than a directive, the GDPR would apply directly and circumvent the need for national implementation, theoretically aiding harmonization. But the legislation stalled for years due to a combination of factors, including aggressive lobbying by US technology companies. As with the Directive before it, geopolitical and commercial considerations provided the necessary motivation to attempt an update.

When the European Commission introduced the Digital Single Market Strategy (DSMS) in 2015, the draft GDPR suddenly shot back to the top of the priority list.[33] In announcing the DSMS, then commission president Jean-Claude Junker noted, "Europe has the capabilities to lead in the global digital economy, but we are currently not making the most of them. Fragmentation and barriers that do not exist in the physical Single Market are holding the EU back."[34] A core barrier outlined in the DSMS was uneven levels of privacy and data protection. Having one data protection law to comply with, rather than twenty-eight different member state laws, coupled with reduced filing and administrative requirements was estimated to save European businesses €2.3 billion annually. Ultimately, the winning proposition was that eliminating barriers to the Digital Single Market could add €415 billion to Europe's GDP.[35] The GDPR was adopted less than a year after this well-articulated business case.

In the two years between its adoption by the European Parliament in 2016 and its entry into force in 2018, the GDPR would become the subject of more international anticipation, analysis, and scrutiny than perhaps any European law before it, in part due to its broad territorial scope. Heralded as a "new law" and reflecting the more expansive reach of digital technologies at the time of its drafting, the GDPR significantly expanded existing data subject rights with respect to information and access, rectification and erasure (also known as the *right to be forgotten*), and the restriction of processing.[36] It also introduced an entirely new right to data portability, enhanced the data subject's right to object to certain processing activities, and expanded rights in relation to automated decision-making and profiling, at least in theory.[37] Importantly, the regulation introduced new requirements for data controllers to undertake a data protection impact assessment for certain high-risk processing activities, and build in core data protection principles and requirements by design and default, shifting some of the burden away from the individual toward the organizations that control and process data. In addition, the GDPR introduced much steeper penalties for noncompliance than the Directive before it.

But the innovations largely ended there. As with the Directive, the GDPR had two primary objectives: to protect the fundamental rights and freedoms of individuals, *and* promote the free movement of personal data across borders—both of equal importance.[38] As such, it outlines multiple lawful bases for processing personal data that account for these sometimes competing objectives, and is not by definition a notice and choice or notice and consent law.[39] Moreover, where processing relies on consent, the GDPR requires that consent to be specific, informed, and unambiguous, evidenced through an affirmative act, easily revocable and freely given, whereas the Directive allowed for mere implicit or opt-out consent. Consent is not freely given where the individual lacks any meaningful choice.[40] In practice, though, much like the Directive before it, the GDPR has, at least to date, largely resulted in an overemphasis on individual consent as a lawful basis for processing personal data in the digital realm—a far more tenuous proposition than it was at the time of the Directive.

By the time the GDPR became law, technological and economic changes driven by digitalization made the world as it was at the time of the Directive almost unrecognizable. Whereas less than 1 percent of the world's population was online in 1995, that number had grown closer to 60 percent. Significantly more people were connected and doing more online. For example, approximately 320 billion emails were sent and more than 500 million Tweets were posted worldwide each day.[41] At the same time, approximately 2.5 quintillion bytes of data were generated daily, accelerated in part by an ever-expanding *Internet of Things* (IoT) universe.[42] Even since the initial draft of the GDPR was introduced in 2012, the proliferation of smart devices and wearables, commercial augmented and *virtual reality* (VR) technologies, AI and machine learning tools, blockchain and decentralized ledger technologies, and other qualitatively new technologies began to spawn a digital universe that was more than doubling in size as well as complexity each year (as further explored in chapter 5).[43]

Despite dramatic technological changes in the intervening decades between the Directive and GDPR, there are vast conceptual similarities between the two. Notably, both instruments are grounded in the international consensus that emerged in the

1970s and 1980s—a consensus born in the early database age. The GDPR's seven core data protection principles correspond closely to the FIPPs—*lawfulness, fairness,* and *transparency* mirror the *transparency* or *openness* principle under the FIPPs, the *purpose limitation* and *storage limitation* principles integrate the FIPPs' *purpose specification* and *use limitation* principles, *data minimization* echoes the *collection limitation* principle, *accuracy* corresponds to *data quality* under the FIPPs, *integrity* and *confidentiality* encompass the *security safeguards* principle under the FIPPs, and finally, the *accountability* principle is common to both frameworks. However relevant these principles remain in theory, the methods for achieving them are stale in practice, particularly when viewed against changes in the scope and capabilities of data-driven technologies and the modern digital economy.

Furthermore, despite seeking to be technology neutral, existing data protection and privacy laws like the GDPR nevertheless exhibit increasingly antiquated views of the digital realm.[44] Like the Directive before it, the GDPR envisages a world made up of neat binaries, wherein lines can be drawn between personal and non-personal data, sensitive and non-sensitive data, anonymous or pseudonymous data, or between data controllers and data subjects. Both laws ultimately presume a world in which individuals interact with known entities primarily through a two-dimensional *graphical user interface* (GUI), such as a computer screen or mobile phone. Through these screens, individuals are meant to be presented with comprehensive written notices about potential uses of their data as well as the opportunity to theoretically make informed assessments and decisions about such uses. But as I will explore, new realities are quickly emerging that challenge this model. As a result of this obsolete framing, coupled with drastically limited resources for comprehensive enforcement, the GDPR has not to date delivered the protections it was anticipated to provide.[45]

Dominant Commercial Interests Undermine Efforts to Update the Law

The GDPR's relative failure to deliver on the high expectations many had for it can be traced to a combination of two primary factors. First, aggressive lobbying by US commercial interests in the drafting and passage of the GDPR, as with many other data-related laws and regulations around the world, has directly diluted its original aims and ambition. And second, due to their ongoing dominance in the global marketplace for digital technologies, US technology companies and platforms have gradually widened the gap between the spirit of data-related laws and regulations as written versus how they are applied in practice. Taken together, as a result of these corporate lobbying efforts and commercial practices, the regulation is so far failing to meet the demands of the modern technological era.

The GDPR has been described as "one of the most lobbied pieces of European legislation in European Union history."[46] Lobbying efforts around the GDPR began even earlier than usual in the life cycle of legislation. Before the first official draft was even published in January 2012, the US Department of Commerce pushed back on the legislative proposal, citing concerns about commercial interoperability as well as its potential impacts on the freedom of expression and cross-border cooperation on consumer protection.[47] US companies also doubled down, concerned about the proposal's heightened requirements for consent, enhanced data subject rights (especially with respect to erasure or the right to be forgotten), new requirements for data portability, additional data breach notification obligations, increased penalties, and revised requirements for cross-border data transfers.[48]

In 2015, Google alone spent more than €3.5 million lobbying Brussels, the highest lobbying budget of any single corporation that year, while also holding the highest number of meetings with top officials from the European Commission of any stakeholder.[49] Its strategy often involved fearmongering, with grand claims to suggest that enacting this type of regulation would be devastating and "Europe's economy will be ruined."[50] In addition to attacking the draft proposal directly, US commercial lobbies leveraged other tools, such as trade negotiations and corporate-funded research and thought leadership from think tanks, to indirectly water it down. As a result of this pressure, the text initially proposed by the commission would be significantly amended even before it could reach the Parliament and European Council for consideration.[51] In this way, through their aggressive lobbying efforts, powerful technology companies ensured that the laws enacted would only ever require what they were already willing to concede.

The GDPR's potential has also been diluted over time by commercial practices and market realities. In principle, the GDPR has a broad territorial scope, applying to all data processing affecting European data subjects regardless of where the processing occurs, or where the data controller or processor is located.[52] With more than five hundred million consumers in the Single Market, companies are incentivized to comply with the regulation to do business in the European Union. In practice, the regulation's reach is even wider due to a kind of *Brussels effect*, whereby large multinational companies wanting access to the European market may decide it would be easier and more cost-effective to adhere to the rules set out in the GDPR and impose them globally across their business operations than it would to establish separate compliance regimes.[53]

But the potential potency of this Brussels effect is weakened in practice by the fact that US corporations exercise substantial control over markets in digital infrastructure and data-driven technologies. For example, Apple and Google jointly control more than 99 percent of the market share for smartphones and operating systems worldwide, dictating what individuals can and cannot do with their devices.[54] US companies also control the $130 billion global cloud market, with Amazon Web Services and Microsoft's Azure alone accounting for more than 50 percent of all cloud services worldwide in 2020.[55] Meta, including its WhatsApp, Instagram, and Facebook Messenger services, remains the largest social network on the planet with nearly three billion active users worldwide, with Google's YouTube in second place.[56] US companies dominate the global market for browsers too, with Google's Chrome taking nearly two-thirds of the worldwide market share alone.[57] Through their ad targeting platforms and services, Meta and Google have a duopoly that controls more than a quarter of all digital advertising spending worldwide.[58]

Due to the ongoing market dominance of large US technology firms, Silicon Valley companies have ended up operationalizing much of the GDPR through their corporate practices, and to put it succinctly, much has been lost in translation. Unfortunately, many of the dominant technology companies that control the data-driven digital environment are US ones that have embraced surveillance capitalism and the related logic of *instrumentarianism*—the orientation of social relations for the modification, prediction, monetization, and control of human behavior.[59] As such, it has been in their interests to dilute the original lofty aims of data protection and privacy laws (designed to enshrine fundamental rights) into a set of policies focused on corporate risk reduction.

Thus the GDPR and many other laws related to data governance have been largely interpreted through the lens of corporate policies revolving around individual privacy in the context of extractive commercial relationships. Privacy scholar Ari Ezra Waldman describes the phenomenon as *privacy managerialism*, whereby privacy is a mere compliance exercise centered on minimizing the law's impact on commercial innovation rather than on substantive adherence to the original aims of privacy law. For Waldman, "Framing privacy obligations in terms of corporate risk focuses only on the avoidance of a corporate problem rather than the achievement of an affirmative social goal—namely, greater user privacy and safety limits on the collection and processing of personal data."[60] This approach has limited the potential reach and impact of laws like the GDPR, and resulted in a distortion of the original spirit and aims of data protection as an extension of the fundamental human right to privacy.

These Distortions Are Replicated the World Over

Despite the limitations of a regulation like the GDPR in theory and practice, the European regulation is often considered to be the gold standard of modern data governance laws. Through an observable Brussels effect, it has inspired dozens of examples of copycat legislation in countries and localities around the world. Some countries, such as Kenya and Uganda, introduced their first-ever national data protection laws in its wake, while others updated or amended existing ones in response. For instance, Argentina introduced a new data protection law in 2018, in part to preserve the adequacy status it first obtained from the European Commission under the Directive in 2003. The GDPR also inspired countries with a previously sectoral approach to data protection, such as India, Nigeria, and Brazil, to shift to a more comprehensive framework. These new and updated laws exhibit a clear influence of the GDPR's core principles and substantive data subject rights, resulting in a kind of global floor for data protection.

Of course, the GDPR's influence is also a function of more direct European strategic and diplomatic efforts to foster a convergence of privacy and data protection laws through various bilateral, regional, and multilateral forums as well as data-related aspects of trade policies. In its proposed comprehensive strategy with Africa, for example, the European Commission laid out several priority areas including digital transformation, strengthening personal

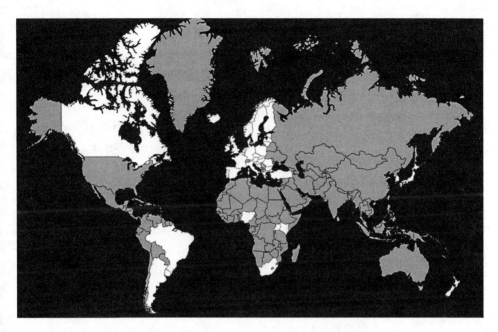

Countries with GDPR-style laws as of May 2021. *Source*: Security Scorecard (https://securityscorecard.com/blog/countries-with-gdpr-like-data-privacy-laws).

data protection, and increasing secure data flows.[61] The commission helped shape data protection and privacy laws in other regions too, including through its participation in a long-standing working group of the Asia-Pacific Economic Cooperation. The desire to protect and promote trade in the digital services market, relying in large part on the free flow of data across national and regional borders, has been a powerful incentive to promote *data protection* even in the absence of underlying conditions that can ensure it remains grounded in human rights rather than economic or commercial incentives.[62]

Unfortunately, to the extent that the GDPR has set a global floor for data governance, it has also risked becoming a kind of global ceiling as many of the regulation's limitations have been exported around the world, tainted and diluted by the same powerful commercial incentives and corporate interests at play in the transatlantic context. As with the GDPR, potentially significant and novel features of these laws—including requirements to undertake ex ante data protection impact assessments, embed data protection requirements into digital processes by design and default, or provide mechanisms for meaningful data portability—have remained underleveraged or unenforced due to commercial realities and other factors outlined above, resulting in a similar kind of compliance-driven managerial privacy as opposed to a genuine human rights–based approach. All the while, data breaches along with the apparent harms of digital tools and technologies have only continued to grow and mount, ratcheting up to a frequency and severity that nearly induced a numbness of the general public to the crisis at hand.[63] In part II, and specifically the next chapter, I examine how the public consciousness reawakened.

II
Data, Data Everywhere

3

The Singular-ity

In spring 2018, it was revealed that Facebook had allowed UK-based political consulting firm Cambridge Analytica to harvest the personal data of up to eighty-seven million Facebook users without their consent for the purposes of psychometric targeting and political advertising. Cambridge Analytica was able to collect the information of users who logged into paid surveys and personality quizzes through their Facebook accounts as well as the personal data of their Facebook friends without their knowledge.[1] The firm was soon identified as central to getting Donald Trump elected in 2016 through "unattributable and untrackable" Facebook advertising campaigns, including the viral "defeat crooked Hillary" along with "lock her up" memes and slogans, and the United Kingdom's decision to leave the European Union.[2]

Unlike traditional data breaches that so many had grown numb to by that point in time, the Cambridge Analytica scandal shook the public psyche, challenging the conventional notion that privacy need not concern those with "nothing to hide." For many, it was the first clear and visceral demonstration of the degree to which personal data could be exploited to track, analyze, and manipulate people for the purpose of engineering high-stakes political outcomes, and also exposed the invasiveness of personal data-driven, targeted, and behavioral advertising practices that fuel the dominant social media platforms and much of the digital economy.[3] In 2019, the popular film *The Great Hack* would retell the Cambridge Analytica story, and explore the dark side of data-hungry social media services like Facebook and Google, breaching the trust between tech companies and consumers in what was termed a *techlash*.[4]

In the wake of the film, cries for help grew louder, marked by a heightened desperation over the state of affairs with regard to data, and a growing consciousness and perception that something was broken or askew in the digital ecosystem, with a profound impact on the American psyche. For example, a 2019 study by the Pew Research Center showed that more than 81 percent of people in the United States felt they had little or no control over the data collected by companies, and the potential risks of such data collection outweighed the benefits, while 79 percent were concerned with how companies use their personal data.[5]

Motivated by a kind of collective outrage and despair over the inability to control how personal data is collected, shared, used, and manipulated, the "data" conversation soon metastasized across corporate boardrooms, legislative offices, academia, international forums such as the G20, and even popular culture. Google searches for *personal data* and the *GDPR* both peaked in May 2018.[6] Around the same time, organizations like the Finland-based MyData, with a mission to "empower individuals by improving their right to self-determination regarding their personal data," would sprout in countries on every continent.[7]

This chapter examines how this shift in the zeitgeist and collective despair around the perceived data governance crisis spurred lawmakers and policymakers, engineers and academics, and entrepreneurs and corporations alike to develop a singular obsession with data as a problem to solve, and how this obsession would galvanize a misguided approach to the governance of digital technologies, leading to further geopolitical fracturing.

Majority of Americans feel as if they have little control over data collected about them by companies and the government

% of U.S. adults who say …

		Companies	The government
Lack of control	They have very little/no control over the data __ collect(s)	**81%**	**84%**
Risks outweigh benefits	Potential risks of __ collecting data about them outweigh the benefits	**81%**	**66%**
Concern over data use	They are very/somewhat concerned about how __ use(s) the data collected	**79%**	**64%**
Lack of understanding about data use	They have very little/no understanding about what __ do/does with the data collected	**59%**	**78%**

Attitudes in the United States toward privacy. *Notes:* Those who did not give an answer or who gave other responses are not shown. Survey titled "Americans and Privacy: Concerned, Confused, and Feeling Lack of Control over Their Personal Information," conducted June 3–17, 2019. *Source:* Pew Research Center (https://www.pewresearch.org/internet/2019/11/15/americans-and-privacy-concerned-confused-and-feeling-lack-of-control-over-their-personal-information).

US Lawmakers Aim to Let People Control Their Data

Alongside the growing popular obsession over data, a flurry of draft laws and regulations related to data protection and privacy were introduced around the world, at every level of government, including in the United States, where momentum for comprehensive privacy legislation had more or less stalled since the 9/11 attacks.

One of the first and most ambitious schemes came in June 2018, when the California legislature passed the California Consumer Privacy Act (CCPA).[8] In fact, the California assembly bill proposing the

CCPA directly cited the Cambridge Analytica scandal, noting, "In March 2018, it came to light that tens of millions of people had their personal data misused by a data mining firm called Cambridge Analytica. . . . As a result, our desire for privacy controls and transparency in data practices is heightened."[9] Despite frequent comparisons to the GDPR, even dubbed by some as a *GDPR lite*, the CCPA is considerably less protective than Europe's law.[10]

Unlike the GDPR, the CCPA does not require a legal or lawful basis for processing personal data. It is also much narrower in scope, excluding health and medical data covered by other sectoral privacy laws, personal information processed by credit reporting agencies, and notably, *publicly available* information. Whereas the GDPR is more proactively focused on the obligations of entities and includes penalties for noncompliance with the regulation, the CCPA is much more concerned with data security and reactive risk mitigation, and only imposes penalties after a breach has occurred. But perhaps most significant is the philosophical divergence between the two. Whereas the GDPR is framed in terms of the fundamental rights of individuals in relation to all entities that process personal data, whether public or private, the CCPA is framed in terms of the commercial relationship between *for-profit companies* and their *consumers* (and only applies to certain businesses based on their revenues or nature of their processing activities).

Shortly after the CCPA became law, and in response to sharp criticisms of its shortcomings, the California legislature adopted the California Privacy Rights and Enforcement Act (CPRA), due to replace the CCPA in 2023.[11] The CPRA expands existing rights and introduces new ones, establishes a new data protection agency, and seeks to make businesses responsible for third-party data processors, among other improvements. Nevertheless, the CCPA remains significant as it was the first state-level omnibus privacy law in the United States to impose broad obligations on businesses across all sectors in an attempt to provide consumers with more transparency and control over personal data, and as a catalyst for similar efforts at both the state and federal level.

The CCPA was soon followed by omnibus legislation in Nevada, Virginia, Colorado, Connecticut, and Utah, alongside comprehensive proposals in a handful of other states.[12] The CCPA also sparked a flurry of other state-level proposals around consumer privacy, broadly construed, including measures related to data brokers, personal information held by *internet service providers*, children's online privacy, website privacy policies, biometric information, data security standards, and more.[13] More than twenty-five states introduced or filed consumer privacy bills in 2019, increasing to thirty states and Puerto Rico in 2020,[14] and thirty-eight states in 2021.[15] Although many proposals failed to survive the legislative process, they nonetheless demonstrated an emerging consensus among the US populace on the need to articulate the rights of consumers and obligations of businesses in relation to data.[16]

Motivated by similar considerations, including the shift in popular sentiment as well as the desire to get ahead of the CCPA and other emerging efforts at the state level, federal proposals for privacy legislation began to proliferate.[17] Congress introduced at least ten federal data privacy proposals in 2018 and 2019. After the COVID-19 pandemic diverted the efforts of the 116th Congress and led to the introduction of pandemic-specific privacy bills in 2020, the 117th Congress reopened the case for federal privacy legislation in 2021 with proposals from members on both sides of the aisle as well as a bipartisan proposal from the House Energy and Commerce Committee.[18] As in the states, additional federal bills were introduced to address related but narrower issues regarding the obligations of internet service providers, facial recognition technology, and children's online privacy, among other topics.

The federal proposals exhibited features of both the CCPA and GDPR, and sometimes a combination of the two, albeit with more US philosophical underpinnings. Most proposals were focused on *consumers* rather than people, varying as to whether consumers have to *opt in* or *opt out* of sharing their data with commercial entities, and introducing new enforcement tools and mechanisms.[19] The vast majority were still predicated on fantasies about individual control over personal data, and grounded in a notice-and-choice or consumer consent-based framework—an increasingly impossible ambition in the face of the scale and growing complexity of the digital environment—thereby making them inherently weak.

Almost all of the proposals adhered to conventional binaries and false dichotomies, such as the separation of *online* and *offline* activities, *personal data* and *non-personal data*, and *sensitive* versus *non-sensitive* data, even as these binaries have failed to hold up in practice. For example, we know that data collected in the physical world, such as through retail beacons, is used to track and manipulate us online, while data collected by digital means is used to track and surveil our physical movements.[20] Similarly, we have seen how grocery store purchases, which are typically not deemed *sensitive* by privacy laws or regulations, can factor into critical decisions about health insurance or social scoring algorithms.[21] We recognize that the line between *personal* and *non-personal data*, which often hinges on the ability to reidentify an individual on the basis of that data, is quickly eroding.

Only a handful of post–Cambridge Analytica proposals had some measure of qualitatively different features. For instance, Senator Brian Schatz (D-HI) proposed the imposition of fiduciary-style duties of care, loyalty, and confidentiality on online service providers with respect to their customers' data, similar to what doctors, lawyers, and other professionals owe their patients and clients, while Senator Sherrod Brown (D-OH) sought to limit data collection and sharing to certain enumerated *permissible purposes*, prohibit the use of personal data for discriminatory purposes, and establish a data protection authority.[22] The limitations of these proposals are perhaps unsurprising given the considerable effort and resources that dominant technology companies and industry consortia have expended through lobbying against strong protections while lobbying *for* watered-down privacy legislation, even drafting the laws themselves in some cases.[23]

Going beyond legislative proposals purportedly aimed at enhancing individual control over personal data processing, some policymakers began calling for a *data dividend* or mechanism for consumers to get paid for the personal data exploited by companies for profit. In the wake of the CCPA, the idea of a data dividend was also entertained by California's then governor Gavin Newsom, who announced he was exploring a way to allow California's consumers to "share in the wealth that is created from their data," failing to explain what that might entail.[24] Without consensus on what a data dividend is or how it might work in practice, proposals ranged from direct payments to individuals in exchange for sharing personal data to more indirect returns to consumers through taxing companies based on their data collection activities.[25] As the market capitalizations of large technology companies like Google and Facebook continued to soar, the data dividend movement captured the public's imagination.

The idea was further popularized by former US Democratic presidential candidate Andrew Yang, who also supported more traditional *universal basic income* schemes. Yang called for treating personal data as property and advocating for rights that at least on the surface, appeared to be GDPR-style data subject rights, including "the right to be informed as to what data will be collected, and how it will be used," "right to opt out of data collection or sharing," "right to be told if a website has data on you, and what that data is," "right to be forgotten; to have all data related to you deleted upon request," and "right to download all data in a standardized format to port to another platform," among others (in other words, rights to information, access, erasure, portability, and more). But unlike fundamental rights in the GDPR, which are inherent and cannot be waived, Yang's policy provided that "you can *waive these rights* and opt in to sharing your data if you wish for the companies' benefit and your own convenience, but then you should receive a share of the economic value generated from your data."[26]

Of course, the United States was not alone in its obsession with data. In some countries, this took the form of new proposals for a *consumer data right* (CDR). Similar to a right to data portability under GDPR-style laws, a CDR gives consumers the right to direct that designated organizations share certain information held about or related to them with accredited third parties. For example, Australia enacted a CDR in August 2019 to initially cover the financial services sector, and eventually extend to the energy and telecommunications sectors.[27] It is aimed at facilitating informed choices by consumers and greater competition between businesses by purporting to provide consumers with better access to, as well as control over, their data. Unlike the fundamental right to data portability in the GDPR, however, the CDR is ultimately a market-based instrument.[28] For instance, under the Australian law, a consumer is defined broadly to include commercial entities, thereby extending the same rights to people and businesses alike.

Even in Europe, where the GDPR was hailed as the pinnacle of a rights-based approach to digital governance, a market-oriented data obsession grew in the shadow of Cambridge Analytica. In 2020, the European Commission introduced a new European strategy for data, including a proposed Data Governance Act (DGA) designed to "foster the availability of data for use by increasing trust in data intermediaries and by strengthening data-sharing mechanisms across the EU."[29] It envisioned new data sharing services aimed at "intermediating between an indefinite number of data holders and users" in new "data-driven ecosystems."[30] The DGA was shortly followed by a proposed Data Act, a draft regulation aimed at "ensuring fairness in the allocation of value from data among actors in the data economy and to foster access to and use of data."[31] Although intended to be without prejudice to fundamental rights laid out in the GDPR, both proposals represent a shift toward the primacy of economic rights and market-based data governance mechanisms, using the language of *users* and *consumers* above *data subjects* or *citizens*.

Europe's data protection authorities immediately raised concerns with the approach set out in both. For example, with respect to the DGA, they observed, "The concept of data sharing service as platform 'intermediating between an indefinite number of data holders and data users' as kind of open data marketplace, would be contrary to . . . data protection principles of privacy by design and by default, transparency and purpose limitation." And with respect to the Data Act, they emphasized the need to comply with the requirements of data protection by design and default. Finally, they cautioned that an overall "policy trend toward a data-driven economy framework without a sufficient consideration of personal data protection aspects raises serious concerns from a fundamental rights viewpoint."[32] Despite these concerns, European lawmakers would advance both proposals.[33]

The Market Seeks to Let People Own, Control, and Even Sell Personal Data

In parallel with efforts by lawmakers, the private sector leveraged popular sentiment and this trend toward a data-driven economy framework for its own commercial opportunities, giving rise to an increasingly crowded marketplace of apps, platforms, and other digital tools promising to help individuals own, control, or even monetize personal data through primarily technological means. Convinced that centralized data collection and storage by large technology companies like Facebook and Google was the root cause of events such as Cambridge Analytica, a flurry of private sector entities and technology start-ups began espousing a rhetoric of *decentralization* as the key to restoring control.[34]

Technologists behind this movement believed that a combination of hardware and software tools, including digital wallets, cryptographic techniques, and advanced computational methods and protocols, could solve the data governance crisis, largely ignoring the social, commercial, and political dimensions of the problem. They preached the gospel of *web 3.0* or *Web3*: the ambition of a decentralized version of the internet powered by peer-to-peer architecture rather than a client-server model, in which data is stored and connected through decentralized protocols, not centralized data repositories.[35] Relying on the use of untested and experimental new technologies such as a distributed database architecture known as *blockchain* or *distributed ledger technology* (DLT), some advocates of decentralization promised a way for individuals to exercise complete control and autonomy over when and how they share personal information about themselves.[36]

For example, internet pioneer Tim Berners-Lee launched a project that would allow individuals to securely store data in decentralized *personal online data stores* (PODs) and authorize trusted data sharing via an open-source software protocol known as Solid.[37] PODs were akin to a digital safe or storage locker for personal data. A POD owner would require websites or other entities to authenticate themselves to an individual before gaining access to data in their POD, and would allow the individual to revoke that access at any time (at least that was the theory since there is no way in practice to force entities from deleting, destroying, or forgetting any data they access).[38] Solid is just one instance of a growing industry of *personal data stores* or *personal data vaults*—a class of technologies that aim to allow individuals to control and monitor access, sharing, and computation over data stored on their personal device, typically a smartphone.[39]

Meanwhile, influential institutions like the World Economic Forum went a step further, advocating for commodity-style data exchanges that would allow individuals to be paid for the use of their personal data.[40] Soon, a host of data marketplaces and data monetization platforms purporting to help people make money by "selling" their personal data burgeoned. For example, the UK-based start-up digi.me introduced the UBDI App (short for *universal basic data income* in a nod to the more traditional notion of a universal basic income), marketed as a tool for "protecting your data, respecting your choices, and making sure you are compensated for the billions of dollars being generated from every swipe, click and step you take!"[41] The UDBI app would allow users to get paid for completing research surveys and studies on topics ranging from sports to travel and more.

Similarly, a Singapore-based foundation promised to kick-start a "New Data Economy" by creating a decentralized, blockchain-based marketplace for selling and exchanging personal data,[42] while another blockchain-based data marketplace purported to allow users to buy and sell personal data streams through self-executing code known as a *smart contract*.[43] Seemingly overnight, specialty data marketplaces emerged allowing people to sell different kinds of personal data, such as location data, health data, and sensitive genomic data, and even to hire out their faces for the creation of deepfakes and other AI tools.[44]

As with the data-centric proposals put forth by lawmakers and policymakers, these commercial initiatives to let people own, control, or monetize personal data suffer from an array of logistical and conceptual shortcomings. As multiple scholars have observed with respect to the data as property analogy, data is quite unlike property in that it is nonrivalrous, nonexcludable, and has a near-zero marginal cost to replicate or reproduce.[45] Moreover, nearly all personal data is in fact interpersonal. As Carissa Véliz notes in *Privacy Is Power*, "Our interdependence in matters of privacy implies that no individual has the moral authority to sell their data. We don't own personal data like we own property because our personal data contains the personal data of others. Your personal data is not only yours."[46]

Another key logistical hurdle to data monetization schemes is the difficulty in pricing personal data given that data points are contextual and also temporal, degrading over time.[47] According to the World Economic Forum and proponents of data monetization schemes, financial incentives would incentivize participation in a marketplace for data, overcoming concerns for privacy or data protection.[48] But evidence suggests that personal data is not nearly as valuable as the public believes it to be. By most recent estimates, the personal data of most individuals retails for well under US$1.[49] For instance, after running an experiment to monetize his data through various decentralized and blockchain-based platforms over several weeks, one technology reporter earned a series of cryptocurrency micropayments worth a grand total of 0.3¢.[50]

Dominant technology companies themselves do not seem to value personal data much more either. On the higher end, Facebook offered teenagers $20 a month to install a virtual private network that gave the company total access to the teens' phones, alarming privacy advocates and attracting regulatory scrutiny.[51] Similarly, Amazon has "paid" people $10 in Amazon credit for their biometric palm prints and $25 in Amazon gift cards for invasive 3D body scans, effectively paying itself.[52] It is hard to argue these are fair exchanges given the significant risks and trade-offs, particularly in light of total uncertainty as to any future uses of that data.

Even putting the commercial realities and logistical challenges aside, there are much bigger concerns in regard to legal, commercial, and technical proposals based on individual ownership, control, and monetization of personal data.

The Poverty of an Overly Individualistic Approach Focused on Data

Given the nature and complexity of the digital world today, it is impossible for an individual to exercise any meaningful control over their experiences through the choices they make with respect to personal data. As early as 2014, a US government report acknowledged that the notion of individual notice and consent had become unworkable as a foundation for consumer privacy enforcement. As the report noted, "Only in some fantasy world do users actually read these notices and understand their implications before clicking to indicate their consent."[53] Given the sheer volume of interactions that feature a digital component today as well as the increasing complexity of the technologies in play, calls for individual control are even more of a fantasy than ever. As we will see in chapter 5, this model is also conceptually misaligned to the emerging postdigital reality we are coming to inhabit.

Privacy professionals and impassioned scholars have long studied and discredited the idea that meaningful privacy protections can be delivered by requiring individuals to exercise more control over their personal information. According to law and computer science professor Woodrow Hartzog, "Privacy regulators and designers have made a mistake by hinging virtually everything on the notion of control."[54] In what he calls the *control illusion*, Hartzog explains that individual control is a finite resource that does not scale. It also risks displacing other crucial objectives like limiting data collection in the first instance. More important, prioritizing control shifts the burden of data governance along with the risks of governance failures and abuses to individuals, hiding the power imbalances that exist in the modern digital economy.

Just as control is an illusion, calls for individual data ownership or monetization would do little to address any of these power dynamics. Instead, they would perpetuate a system in which each individual, acting alone, makes a series of concessions that feel inconsequential in isolation, but that over time and in the aggregate across many individuals, result in a gradual yet monumental ceding of power to the already powerful. Moreover, paying individuals to share their personal data would add further financial incentives to this surrendering of power. As Shoshana Zuboff argues, "It is obscene to suppose that this harm can be reduced to the obvious fact that users receive no fee for the raw material they supply. That critique is a feat of misdirection that would use a pricing mechanism to institutionalize and therefore legitimate the extraction of human behavior for manufacturing and sale."[55]

As we are coming to recognize, the technology governance challenges we face today are fundamentally about power—the steep asymmetries of power between people and corporations as well as people and their governments (and increasingly, between governments and corporations), the wielding of power and way that decisions about its wielding are made, and threats posed to the fundamental rights of individuals by their ever-diminishing degree of power in the face of increasingly complex and opaque technologies like AI, advanced machine learning methods, and algorithmic decision-making.[56] Hyperindividualistic approaches focused almost exclusively on technical tools or data would only sanction as well as cement the existing asymmetries of knowledge, capacity, and power that have eroded the rights of individuals, and veer us further down the path of commodifying human experience vis-à-vis data.

These hyperindividualistic approaches to data governance are antisocial in contravention of general principles of law and policy. Deriving from the human right to privacy, data protection seeks to balance individual rights and interests against those of the public writ large, recognizing that there are times when the latter must prevail. This is why laws consistently offer more than one basis for processing data, including alternatives to individual consent as well as exceptions and derogations in the interests of others and society as a whole. Neoliberal proposals based on the primacy of individual ownership or control over data are at odds with this conception of data protection rooted in international human rights law—a body of law that recognizes the interrelatedness of, and seeks to reconcile tensions between, often competing rights. They are misaligned with non-Western values and cultures too, such as more collective traditions organized around Confucian or Ubuntu ethics. Finally, data-centric, individualistic approaches are ill-suited for increasingly collective challenges that require cross-border collaboration and consensus, and serve to distract us from the original aims of data protection—namely protecting people.

More Collective Approaches Emerge but Still Suffer from an Obsession with Data

Recognizing the limits of an individualistic view of data protection and privacy, a variety of newer proposals emphasize a more collective approach to data governance. Despite the many permutations of these proposals, some of the more popular among them fall into three categories: efforts to establish collective or pooled rights and interests in data through the formation of new entities such as data unions, data cooperatives, and data trusts; efforts to enhance and enable data sharing through the creation of new zones such as data commons, data banks, or other common data spaces; and a miscellany of technical projects that build new technological tools for collective or shared data management. As none of these proposals has broad traction in practice at this stage, the definitions and uses of these terms are still evolving. Nevertheless, it is worth evaluating each emerging trend as well as their relative advantages and disadvantages.

The notion of a *data union* typically stems from a view of data as labor or the product of a kind of human effort that is akin to labor.[57] As with a labor union, a data union would serve as a collective bargaining tool for people who are *laboring* by creating data. The idea is that such a union could negotiate with large tech companies for better terms and even better *wages* for people with respect to the data they create. Data unions are sometimes alternatively referred to as *data cooperatives*, though they are largely the same idea, whereby members of a data union or cooperative cede a degree of autonomy over decision-making and control to the entity. Similarly, a *data trust* typically refers to a legal structure that is designed to provide independent stewardship of some data set for the benefit of certain people or organizations.[58] A data union or cooperative may or may not form such a data trust for the stewardship of its members' data.

The core innovation of data unions, cooperatives, or trusts is that they treat data as a pooled resource rather than an individual one. Yet some of the key challenges with these new entities include how to avoid the same problems posed by existing ecosystem intermediaries, how to fund them without risking their independence, and how to determine their permissible purposes. For example, should we allow data unions to form if they would ultimately help individuals skirt regulations in the way that creative legal entities and charitable vehicles have in other contexts? As a matter of public policy, should we allow the establishment of data trusts with the primary purpose of profit maximization or data unions with the mission of obtaining a higher price for the personal data of their members?

The second category of innovations is concerned with the creation of new spaces, typically in the form of a *data commons*, alternatively known as a *data bank*. These proposals are less concerned with collective bargaining, and more focused on enhancing and enabling data sharing as well as facilitating broad access to data, while respecting individual privacy and data protection. In its 2020 communication, "A European Strategy on Data," the European Commission proposed the creation of EU-wide *common data spaces* in various sectors, including manufacturing, health, financial services, and energy,[59] which would later form part of the Data Governance Act. The idea behind these spaces is to pool sector-specific data into a *common data space* or *public data bank* that individuals or organizations could access for a broad array of purposes, including research or innovation. In this way, these proposals are also designed to prevent the monopolization of data as a common resource. Data commons raise all the traditional concerns about any common resource, including how to avoid a tragedy of the commons.[60]

While these solutions improve on the status quo by going beyond individualism in some respects, such as by attempting to address asymmetrical power or improving access to data to prevent monopolization, they can still only ever be partial solutions. The creation of new entities that live by the existing market-based rules can only enable incremental improvements for people. For example, the members of a data union might negotiate some payment in exchange for data, but they would still have little say over what a purchaser ultimately does with it. And just as labor unions are no substitute for labor or employment law, data unions are no substitute for effective data governance. Likewise, the creation of new data spaces, while curbing some of the market power of private sector entities that may be forced to share their data, does not change the fundamentals of the market or rules with respect to data. Worse yet, these ideas could create in-groups and out-groups, providing enhanced protections for some and more limited protections for others depending on, for instance, the quality of one's data union or the interoperability or transferability of any data shared.

None of the collective proposals explored here would stop nefarious and harmful data practices, enhance or augment the rights of individuals against emerging practices that may further threaten their freedom and autonomy, or address what the rules or norms with respect to data should be. In many ways, they actually support the status quo by sanctioning the continued treatment of personal data as a commodity and human experience as a raw material for commercial extraction. Thus these measures are largely still market-based solutions to problems with important nonmarket dimensions. Ultimately, however, these more collective approaches fail for a much less apparent reason: they are still largely organized around the notion of *data*.

The next chapter explores how powerful technology companies have weaponized this singular obsession with data to erode the original aims of data protection and privacy laws in ways that put people at heightened risk.

4

(Data) Privacy, the Handmaiden

In the wake of Cambridge Analytica and the ensuing techlash, dominant technology companies amped up their public relations campaigns around privacy, including by calling on lawmakers and policymakers to enact new "privacy" laws and regulations. Despite this dramatic shift in rhetoric painting grand visions of privacy as a fundamental human right, the actual strategies adopted by these companies revealed a narrower, more technical conception of privacy as control over the confidentiality and security of data—a version of privacy they helped enshrine in data-centric laws and regulations.

In response to public sentiment along with a legal crackdown on data collection and processing activities, big tech would increasingly rely on technological solutions and mathematical methods of skirting the spirit of new laws. As laws focused on data collected directly from users, companies began to depend more on data indirectly obtained, observed, and inferred by other means, including through the use of AI and machine learning tools. Similarly, as many laws revolved around the relationship between companies and their customers as consumers, companies could collect or infer data from outside this commercial relationship through data brokers, government records, and other public sources. And as laws continued to distinguish between personal and non-personal data, companies increasingly sought to leverage aggregation, anonymization, and deidentification techniques to continue to extract insights and exert control.

In turn, this narrow view of privacy, supported by a reliance on technological tools and methods, would help companies preach the gospel of privacy, while sustaining their extractive operations and supporting the status quo, all the while allowing them to further consolidate power vis-à-vis individuals and governments alike. Challenger firms branding themselves as part of Web3 or the metaverse would espouse a similarly narrow and technical view of privacy, repeating many of the same mistakes as (and ultimately bolstering) the incumbents. This chapter explores how industry's reconceptualization of privacy as a technical exercise in confidentiality and control over data risks transforming the once-powerful notion of privacy into the handmaiden of corporate surveillance and control.

Big Tech Goes on a Privacy PR Offensive

In a 2018 keynote address at the fortieth annual International Conference of Data Protection and Privacy Commissioners in Brussels—a high-profile, highly influential conference for data protection regulators and authorities from around the world—Apple CEO Tim Cook prominently proclaimed, "We at Apple believe that privacy is a fundamental human right," and condemned the burgeoning "data industrial complex" whereby "information, from the everyday to the deeply personal, is being weaponized against us with military efficiency."[1] Soon thereafter, Apple rolled out slogans such as "Your data, Your choice," alongside new privacy features such as its App Tracking Transparency tool requiring apps to request opt-in consent from users prior to tracking them across other apps and websites.[2]

Apple also made waves in Las Vegas at the 2019 Consumer Electronics Show, one of the biggest and most influential consumer technology conferences in the world, with the launch of an ad campaign featuring building-sized billboards that read, "What happens on your iPhone, stays on your iPhone."[3] The campaign was seen by many as a swipe at Facebook and Google, and an attempt by Apple to differentiate itself from competitors based on its privacy practices. Although Apple led the charge on privacy as a competitive advantage, other tech titans would soon follow suit, launching privacy-focused PR offensives of their own.

Like Apple, Microsoft promised to "fight for legal protection of your privacy as a fundamental human right," while continuing to articulate a vision of privacy based on user control through "easy-to-use tools and clear choices."[4] In May 2018, Microsoft announced that it would voluntarily extend the GDPR's data subject rights to all of its customers worldwide and introduced a privacy dashboard to give users the "tools they need to take control of their data," as it lobbied for federal privacy legislation at home.[5] In an op-ed in the *Hill*, Microsoft's chief privacy officer called on Congress to enact a federal privacy law to give consumers "control over their data," while cautioning that "a U.S. law should not copy the GDPR."[6] All the while, Microsoft played an active role in pushing state-level legislative proposals far weaker than the GDPR in Washington, Arizona, Hawaii, Illinois, and Minnesota—proposals criticized by privacy advocates and consumer groups as "full of loopholes."[7]

In March 2019, exactly one year after the Cambridge Analytica revelations, Zuckerberg penned an op-ed in the *Washington Post* calling for updated rules for the internet with respect to harmful content, election integrity, data portability, and privacy. In it, he advocated for "comprehensive privacy legislation in line with the European Union's General Data Protection Regulation" and emphasized that it should "protect your right to choose how your information is used,"[8] all the while continuing to move billions of users out of the GDPR's territorial reach to avoid compliance.[9]

A month later, at Facebook's annual developer conference, Zuckerberg raised eyebrows by declaring, "The future is private," despite the company's well-cataloged history of privacy abuses. Zuckerberg elaborated on his vision in writing, explaining, "I believe the future of communication will increasingly shift to private, encrypted services where people can be confident what they say to each other stays secure and their messages and content won't stick around forever."[10] In other words, his vision of *privacy* had to do with secure, confidential communications through apps owned and controlled by Facebook rather than *privacy* as a fundamental human right.

From 2018 to 2019, Google also amplified its privacy PR efforts, and doubled down on the rhetoric of choice and control in a move that some referred to as Google's "pivot to privacy."[11] It announced a series of changes to its products and services, all in the name of user "privacy," including updated settings and controls for its Google Analytics products, the discontinuation of its emergency location-sharing app, adjustments to its *application programming interface* (API) permissions for browser extensions, and the eventual phaseout of third-party cookies in its Chrome Browser.[12] In a *New York Times* op-ed, Google CEO Sundar Pichai wrote, "To make privacy real, we give you clear, meaningful choices around your data," and took aim at Apple by adding, "Privacy cannot be a luxury good offered only to people who can afford to buy premium products and services." Like Zuckerberg, he expressed support for comprehensive federal privacy legislation to create "consistent and universal protections for individuals and society as a whole."[13]

Alongside their PR operations, dominant technology companies would publicly claim to support comprehensive federal privacy legislation in the United States, all the while lobbying against meaningful efforts and supporting watered-down legislative proposals behind the scenes.[14] Even Amazon's then CEO Jeff Bezos joined the public chorus, signing a letter alongside fifty other CEOs from the Business Roundtable calling on the US Congress to pass a federal privacy law, while Amazon worked to whittle down draft legislation in its home state of Washington.[15] Yet despite these lofty claims about privacy as a fundamental right, industry's actions suggested a different and much less expansive interpretation of privacy.

Big Tech Adopts PETs

Alongside its rhetorical offensive, big tech enthusiastically embraced and adopted so-called *privacy-preserving* or *privacy-enhancing technologies* (PETs) to reassure the public, give the appearance of complying with existing laws and regulations, and attempt to stave off more aggressive legal and regulatory interventions. While there is no single definition or standard for what constitutes a PET, the term is typically used to refer to a wide array of technical means, tools, and approaches that can help mitigate data privacy and security risks, such as the risk of revealing sensitive attributes present in a data set.[16] Popular examples of PETs include cryptographic protocols such as homomorphic encryption and secure multiparty computation; anonymization techniques such as differential privacy; methods for pseudonymization, obfuscation, and data masking, such as zero knowledge proofs; on-device machine learning techniques such as federated learning; and synthetic data generation.

For example, in 2018, Amazon began using the phrase *privacy-aware data processing* to describe how it integrates "state-of-the-art privacy-enhancing technologies" into all of its products and services.[17] Specifically, Amazon promoted its use of *differential privacy*—an anonymization technique developed in the early 2000s that aims to reduce the likelihood of harmful data disclosures or malicious uses of data by injecting mathematical *noise* to obscure individual identities in a given database or data set.[18] Amazon explained how it uses differential privacy to ensure that its machine learning algorithms can observe frequent patterns in data without memorizing details about any specific individual, allowing the company to ensure that "customer data is protected through the entire process of ingestion, transportation, storage, and finally processing and modelling."[19] Note the emphasis on protecting *customer data* rather than *customers*.

In an attempt to restore trust in its products and services, Google began to communicate and underscore its use of federated machine learning, differential privacy, and other PETs to promote its version of user privacy.[20] In 2019, for instance, Google announced the *Privacy Sandbox*—a project to explore replacements for third-party cookie-based advertising in a "secure environment for personalization that also protects user privacy," along with a host of other technical proposals for open standards to enhance privacy on the web.[21] While Firefox, Safari, and other browsers phased out third-party cookies years earlier, the announcement sent shock waves through the digital advertising industry, which had relied on cookies and other trackers to target and retarget behavioral ads to people, due to Google's control of nearly two-thirds of the global browser market.

The Privacy Sandbox would rely on a number of PETs, including a technique known as *federated learning* whereby a machine learning algorithm analyzes decentralized data locally stored on individual devices by only transmitting insights gleaned back to the centralized model.[22] For example, Google initially proposed an unsupervised machine learning algorithm known as the *Federated Learning of Cohorts* (FLoC) for clustering people into groups for ad targeting based on their recent browsing history. It would essentially enable the Chrome browser to collect information about a user's browsing habits, assign the user to a *cohort* or group of users with similar habits, attach a *cohort ID* to that group, and then share that ID with websites and advertisers. Instead of cookies or direct access to users' personal information, advertisers could then use these tools to target ads through Google's browser-based APIs.[23]

Just as Google embraced browser-based PETs through its Privacy Sandbox, Apple and Google embraced PETs to enable a shift from cloud-based data processing activities to local, device-based data processing. The device duopoly, which together controls more than 99 percent of the total global market for smartphones, promoted the use of on-device machine learning and computational methods designed to mitigate the privacy and security risks of transmitting data to the cloud.[24] For instance, at its 2021 Worldwide Developers Conference, Apple debuted the *Apple Neural Engine*, an on-device machine learning tool that enables its Siri voice assistant to process requests on an iPhone or iMac without transmitting the data to Apple's servers.[25] And around the same time, Google introduced the *Private Compute Core* for its Android devices, which similarly uses on-device machine learning to process audio and language in a partitioned space within the Android operating system.[26]

While dominant smartphone manufacturers like Apple and Google sought to leverage PETs locally on devices, enterprise-focused companies with substantial cloud-based infrastructure and revenue streams embraced PETs as a way to promote trust and confidence in cloud-based processing capabilities in the face of growing concerns about the privacy and security of data stored as well as processed remotely in the cloud. Top cloud service providers, including Amazon, Microsoft, and IBM, began to endorse *confidential computing*—experimental methods for protecting the security and privacy of data while in use by performing computation in a hardware-based *trusted execution environment*—as a way to persuade customers to transfer more data and functions to the cloud.[27]

And where promises and assurances about the privacy and security of data, whether locally on a device or remotely in the cloud, were still insufficient to overcome regulatory or commercial concerns, another PET known as *synthetic data* started to surge in popularity. Synthetic data is computer-generated data designed as a stand-in for real-world data and is being used to provide data sets to power AI tools for the finance, healthcare, insurance, and other industries. Synthetic data can also be used to generate "noise" for differentially private data sets, as in the case of Microsoft's Smart-Noise system, demonstrating how different PETs are frequently used in combination.[28] These examples also show the many ways in which PETs can be used to support existing business models and operations.

The Problem with PETs

While PETs are not new, they have been surging in popularity since the data-focused shift in the zeitgeist. In fact, PETs can be traced back to as early as 1995, when a report jointly authored by the information and privacy commissioner of Ontario and the Dutch Data Protection Authority examined their use to promote anonymity in online transactions.[29] After decades of slow industry adoption due to high implementation costs, computational limits, and other resource constraints, PETs began to be embraced as companies sought to adapt to the GDPR, CCPA, and an array of new data-focused rules and regulations around the world.[30]

To a degree, PETs can help achieve compliance with these laws and regulations, particularly when combined with information security–related policies and procedures, personnel management and access controls, record keeping, audits, and other organizational measures. The GDPR, for example, requires entities to implement data protection by design and default through both organizational and technical measures, including the use of *state-of-the-art* technological processes.[31] As a result, PETs are a rapidly growing market attracting considerable interest and investment from enterprises large and small.[32] They are also part of a growing trend by the big tech companies to suggest that the solution to technology-related privacy challenges is in fact more technology.

Despite their promise and growing demand, PETs are far from perfect. For one thing, they can be highly technical, complex, and difficult to use, and often have confusing user interfaces. This can result in errors that actually undermine individual privacy and security.[33] They are also expensive and resource intensive, frequently requiring large data sets and computing power, making them off-limits for many smaller market participants.[34] For instance, some of the newest and more advanced PETs are often available only to entities that already wield disproportionate power over the digital environment through vast troves of data, infrastructure, and computational resources (here it is worth noting that companies with the historically most data-intensive practices are now among the most fervent advocates and adopters of PETs).

Due to complexity and resource limitations, PETs can be notoriously difficult for lawmakers and policymakers to audit or govern too. For example, while data protection authorities can conduct *cookie sweeps* to audit a company's compliance with cookie-related laws and regulations, they lack similar tools for companies using PET-enabled tracking tools and would have trouble, say, auditing Google's federated machine learning algorithm for data protection compliance.[35] This opacity, in turn, presents challenges to accountability over these tools and how they are wielded. Moreover, given the lack of a common definition or standards for PETs, it can be difficult to evaluate the efficacy of any given tool or technique in a specific context. Despite potential gains with respect to the privacy and security of data through PETs, there are significant trade-offs concerning accuracy, fairness, robustness, explainability, and even security. Finally, there is evidence that PETs, like differential privacy, merely shift privacy and security risks from external to internal threats, such as by incentivizing insider attacks over more traditional cybercrimes such as hacking.[36]

This combination of usability challenges, resource constraints, and accountability hurdles means that PETs can engender a false sense of safety or security, while introducing new privacy and security risks.[37] These false assurances, in turn, could actually incentivize more data collection, sharing, and processing, undermining core data protection principles like data minimization and storage limitation. For example, an internal presentation from an industry consortium established to develop and promote methods as well as standards for confidential computing details how it aims to "enable new public cloud scenarios [such as] migrating extremely sensitive data to the cloud, and enabling multi-party sharing scenarios that have been difficult to build due to privacy, security, and regulatory requirements" in order to "[promote] investment across the value chain."[38] In other words, it acknowledges that confidential computing could actually incentivize *more* data sharing and encourage more value extraction.

But even where PETs succeed with data minimization and do not result in sharing more personal data, they can legitimize activities that many would otherwise find objectionable or concerning, and frequently with more efficiency. Google's "privacy pivot" through the use of federated learning, for instance, may not actually protect individual privacy or prevent individual users from being tracked, even as it raises a host of other concerns.[39] As the Electronic Frontier Foundation cautioned with respect to Google's proposal, "FLoC is designed to prevent a very specific threat: the kind of individualized profiling that is enabled by cross-context identifiers today. . . . But even if Google is able to iterate on its design and prevent these risks, the harms of targeted advertising are not limited to violations of privacy. FLoC's core objective is at odds with other civil liberties."[40] Those harms include discrimination, harassment, exclusion, and exploitation, among others. After significant backlash over its original FLoC proposal, Google continued to introduce substantially similar proposals that would merely reduce the number of interest groups or categories associated with an individual user, leaving many of the same criticisms intact.[41]

It is also important to consider the role of a technique such as differential privacy in enabling or exacerbating private control over infrastructure, as in the case of Amazon's use of big data to control supply chains and map entire urban environments. Amazon gives the illustration of "using differentially private machine learning to analyze the commuting patterns of individuals within a city [without] remembering the commute patterns of any specific individual."[42] Similarly, advertising technology vendors and digital marketers are embracing the use of differential privacy to derive aggregate insights about consumers without revealing information about any specific individual consumer, while still enabling invasive ad targeting and personalization.[43] And digital identity providers are using homomorphic encryption for cloud-based verification as well as biometric identity verification and authentication based on facial images that may be scraped from public sources without consent.[44] Examples of PETs used to legitimate problematic ends abound.

PETs can also help companies sidestep data-focused privacy laws entirely. Take the use of synthetic data for purposes or ends that would be impermissible or off-limits with the use of personal data. For instance, Israeli synthetic data company Datagen offers synthetic data sets for a variety of use cases such as generating facial expressions to monitor driver alertness or distraction in smart cars, simulating human body motions and object interactions to track customers in cash-free stores, blink analysis and gaze tracking to improve the capabilities of VR headsets, and drone monitoring. It markets its products to its customers as "free[ing them] from the headaches of manual data acquisition, annotation, and cleaning."[45] But as one scholar notes, "Just because the data is 'synthetic' and does not directly correspond to real user data does not mean that it does not encode sensitive information about real people."[46]

Moreover, synthetic data is still built on real-world data at the source.[47] Nevertheless, using synthetic data allows companies to offer cheap and efficient surveillance tools, often without triggering personal data or privacy-related regulations.

Just as ending third-party cookies does not end behavioral targeting and tracking, processing data locally rather than in the cloud does not prevent unfair or discriminatory outcomes imposed by means of algorithmic processes and automated decision-making. Similarly, protecting data while it is remotely processed in the cloud, as in the case of confidential computing, does not prevent harmful or nefarious uses of that data in the real world. In fact, by enabling and incentivizing more data sharing between companies, it further deepens the asymmetries as between individuals and private entities, further consolidating power in industry. Instead of increasing the privacy of individuals, privacy-preserving verifiable attribute-based digital identity credentials actually create more incentives and opportunities for function creep, tracking, and profiling.[48] And finally, as opposed to preventing the development of surveillance tools and infrastructure, synthetic data actually makes it cheaper and easier to do so.

In other words, where the law sets out a hurdle to the use of any given kind of data, there is also a PET that promises to decrease or circumvent such hurdles so that companies can continue to carry out the same activities they have always undertaken. As scholar Michael Veale observes, "Data is just a means to an end, and new, cryptographic tools are emerging that let those firms' same potentially problematic ends be reached without privacy-invasive means. These tools give those controlling and coordinating millions or even billions of computers the monopolistic power to analyse or shape communities or countries, or even to change individual behaviour, such as to privately target ads based on their most sensitive data—without any single individual's data leaving their phone."[49] So are we better off?

Distorting Privacy Helps Tech Consolidate Power

These examples also demonstrate how technology companies are using PETs and other technologies to superficially follow the letter of data-focused laws while simultaneously violating their spirit. For example, as many data protection laws hinge on the identifiability of individuals, industry is embracing PETs for anonymization, deidentification, pseudonymization, and obfuscation. But academic researchers have repeatedly demonstrated the degree to which deidentification, anonymization, and aggregation do not reliably prevent reidentification, and even where they do, privacy and security risks remain, particularly with respect to certain groups and communities.[50] For example, the fitness tracking app Strava made headlines for revealing the location and activities of US military personnel around clandestine bases in Syria when it published anonymized heat maps of popular running routes.[51] These types of risks are not solved with the use of differential privacy or other anonymization techniques, which only achieve a narrow, mathematical view of privacy.

In fact, PETs are allowing dominant technology companies to reimagine privacy in their own self-interested image. For example, at Facebook's 2019 developer conference, Zuckerberg said, "Over time . . . a private social platform will be even more important to our lives than our digital town squares."[52] As with his "the future is private" declaration, Zuckerberg was painting a vision of privacy that is focused on private communications infrastructure owned and controlled by Facebook. Similarly, Apple's "What happens on your iPhone, stays on your iPhone" campaign, criticized by privacy advocates for misrepresenting the company's record on privacy, reveals Apple's increasing tendency to conflate privacy and the confidentiality of data stored on its devices.[53] Even if data remains locally stored and processed on an individual's device, it can still be used to manipulate their behavior and engineer certain outcomes in ways that intrude on the personal boundaries and autonomy that privacy traditionally seeks to protect. And Google's shift from third-party tools to greater dependence on its first-party ecosystem suggests a similar view of privacy as confidentiality or secrecy vis-à-vis third parties rather than from Google itself.[54]

Perhaps even more significantly, these moves signal a broader shift toward the enclosure of digital spaces through ever-expanding, privately owned *walled gardens* or digital fiefdoms governed by opaque automated tools. For instance, rather than ending tracking, Google's new "privacy" tools would merely enable it through more opaque methods within Google's own ecosystem.[55] In fact, all the proposals in Google's Privacy Sandbox would actually channel more and more activity into Google's own first-party ecosystem, routing everything through Google's APIs and automated tools, and increasing third-party reliance on Google. Viewed through this lens, it becomes apparent how Google's planned phaseout of third-party cookies is no skin off its back when it can be the first and only party shaping user behavior through the Chrome browser. Indeed, the title of Google's original announcement captures it best: "Building a More Private Web."[56] And Google is not alone.

Apple's new "privacy" tools and features similarly deepen its dominance through the company's control over infrastructure, such as mobile hardware- and software-based operating systems. In line with its general push toward localized machine learning, Apple introduced the new iCloud Privacy Relay tool, which is designed to stop websites from building a profile of you by preventing them from matching your website requests with your actual IP address, and App Tracking Transparency tool, which requires apps to request permission before tracking users.[57] Both tools actually deepen Apple's vertical integration into digital advertising markets by routing app developers and advertisers through Apple's ecosystem, without limiting Apple's access to advertising data. Similarly, Apple's introduction of a digital identity feature, which allows users to store driver's licenses and other identity credentials through the Apple Wallet, in much the same way as Apple Pay, will only make Apple users more dependent on and tethered to their iPhones as the device becomes a one-stop shop for payments, identification, communications, and more. In fact, these privacy moves have triggered anticompetitive accusations against Apple from competitors and scrutiny from regulators around the world.[58]

Distorting Privacy Also Threatens the Public Sphere

A distorted notion of privacy as confidentiality or control over data is incentivizing companies to bring more into their own ecosystems, deepen their vertical integration, build higher walls to keep competitors out, and use privacy as a shield against competition. When privacy is reduced to the mere privacy, confidentiality, and security of *data*, there are virtually no limits to what these companies can do or the activities they can undertake, as long as they safeguard and secure any data they process along the way. In this way, these measures merely protect the privacy and security of *data* at the expense of the privacy and security of *people*, who continue to be vulnerable to control, manipulation, and exploitation by entities wielding unprecedented power. As a result of these distorted notions of privacy, dominant technology firms do not only gain significant power over people. Rather, as they easily circumvent data-related limitations and continue to accumulate resources and control over critical infrastructure, these firms introduce commercial incentives into all facets of life in a way that threatens to erode the public sphere.

The public controversy over technologies deployed during the COVID-19 pandemic—so called *pandemic tech*—provides an additional illustration of the problem. At the start of the pandemic, the public conversation over mobile phone–based *contact tracing* or *exposure notification apps* purporting to track and trace the spread of the virus quickly narrowed in on designing and deploying such apps in a manner that would preserve and protect individual privacy. Specifically, the debate focused on whether these apps should be "centralized" or "decentralized," in the sense of whether data collected should be stored and processed in a remote, centralized server or else locally on individuals' devices, respectively. While the centralized model was arguably more valuable for insights that it could provide epidemiologists and public health authorities with respect to the spread of COVID-19, the decentralized model was touted as more "privacy preserving" by limiting governments' ability to repurpose data to surveil populations.

Apple and Google quickly began to build and deploy a self-described "privacy-preserving" exposure notification app of the decentralized variety utilizing differential privacy, secure computation protocols, localized data processing, secret sharing, zero knowledge proofs, and a variety of other PETs to enable computation and analytics on aggregated metrics.[59] They claimed their app was privacy preserving because it was "designed so that the identities of the people a device comes into contact with are protected."[60] In other words, they equated privacy with confidentiality.

Through their global market dominance over hardware devices and software operating systems as well as their ability to move faster than democratic governments could come to a consensus on their approach, these private companies would even prevent governments from introducing alternatives.[61] Unsurprisingly, many lawmakers would end up privileging individual privacy over any potential epidemiological insights. More than a year into the pandemic, the efficacy of these tools remained an open question, even as the technical infrastructure would continue to be embedded in the operating systems of most smartphones.[62]

A similar phenomenon would unfold later in the pandemic. As vaccinations were developed and rolled out, the public debate

Alice and Bob don't know each other but have a lengthy conversation sitting a few feet apart.

Bob is positively diagnosed for COVID-19 and enters the test result in an app from his public health authority.

Their phones exchange beacons with random Bluetooth identifiers (which change frequently).

A few days later...

With Bob's consent, his phone uploads the last 14 days of keys for his Bluetooth beacons to the server.

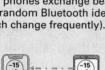

Apps can only get more information via user consent.

~14 day temporary store

 | Google

Alice continues her day unaware she had been near a potentially contagious person.

Alice receives a notification on her phone.

ALERT: you have recently come in contact with someone who has tested positive for COVID-19.

Tap for more information -->

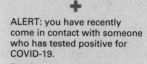

Alice's phone periodically downloads the Bluetooth beacon keys of everyone who has tested positive for COVID-19 in her region. A match is found with Bob's random Bluetooth identifiers.

Sometime later...

Alice's phone receives a notification with information about what to do next.

A match is found.

Additional information is provided by the health authority app.

Anonymous identifier keys are downloaded periodically.

 | Google

Visual depiction of Apple and Google's "privacy-preserving" contact tracing/expo sure notification app introduced during the COVID-19 pandemic. *Source*: Apple (https://covid19-static.cdn-apple.com/applications/covid19/current/static/contact -tracing/pdf/ExposureNotification-FAQv1.2.pdf).

shifted from contact tracing and exposure notification apps, to COVID-19 *immunity certificates* or *vaccine passports* purporting to enable individuals to present a digital certificate or credential intended to prove that they have been vaccinated against, tested negative for, or recovered from the virus. As with contact tracing apps, governments and key stakeholders quickly zeroed in on the privacy risks of vaccine passports while hardly considering the degree to which these digital tools could even further their stated public health objectives, even as the World Health Organization cast doubts on their effectiveness.[63] And as the private sector took the lead in rolling out vaccine passports in countries around the world, its promises about the privacy and security of any data collected by these apps eclipsed conversations about the legitimacy of introducing these tools, the precedent they would set, or the relative balance of power as between the public and private sector.[64]

Privacy Risks Becoming a Handmaiden of Surveillance and Control

While there are good reasons to embrace PETs that are proven to work, there are also good reasons to be suspicious when these tools are embraced by some of the most powerful companies on the market—companies that are implementing and embedding infrastructures to surveil as well as control the behavior of individuals, groups, and entire communities. As these examples illustrate, big tech's rhetorical shift and strategic adoption of PETs and other measures taken in the name of "privacy" are actually helping it preserve and consolidate power in the face of a governance crackdown narrowly focused on data. Such measures allow these companies to preach the gospels of privacy and security without changing the fundamentals of their business models, altering their core activities, or ceding any power or control, all the while putting individuals and communities at risk.

Big tech's embrace of PETs demonstrates how easily impoverished notions of privacy centered on *data* can be weaponized by industry to serve an agenda of domination, control, and extraction—in other words, to perpetuate the status quo. As the popularity of PETs shows, *data* protection or *data* privacy are not the same as protection or privacy for people, despite frequent conflation of the two. Distracted by these tools, we risk losing sight of the original aims of privacy—to maintain zones or spheres around the inner or private life of the individual; protect the individual's physical person, home, and family life; create boundaries that are foundational to the exercise and enjoyment of other fundamental rights and freedoms; protect individuals from discrimination and harassment; and ultimately, defend the individual liberty and autonomy necessary for a fully functioning democracy.

In fact, the more that our laws continue to concentrate on requiring companies to protect the privacy and security of *data*, the more we forget to protect the privacy and security of *people*. In this way, the rising popularity of PETs also exposes some of the deficiencies in our data-centric legal frameworks that focus on the *means* rather than the *ends*, akin to outlawing the murder weapon (such as behavioral engineering based on personal data) over murder itself (i.e., behavioral engineering), by whatever means. Meanwhile, controlling firms will just use another weapon to achieve the same ends, as demonstrated by the use of synthetic data for purposes that would be otherwise impermissible with the use of personal data. As companies continue to find ways to move beyond data, so too must our approach to governing digital tools and technologies—this is the subject of the next and final part of this book.

III
Beyond Data

5
A Brave New World

In a hype-making 2019 report titled *The Post-Digital Era Is upon Us*, global consulting firm Accenture described the reality of digital technologies as ubiquitous across industry and "the price of admission for doing business." According to Accenture, the term *digital* is passé, and "the days of calling something digital to insinuate that it is new and innovative are numbered."[1] In fact, as everything becomes increasingly digital, the digital world approximates the world. Such a postdigital reality has significant implications for how we ought to think about laws and policies for technology governance, including data-hungry technologies that we have historically attempted to govern indirectly by way of data.

Plainly, the future of "data governance" as a tool of technology governance is not actually about data. Rather, it is about an imminent future with the internet in everything—a new cyberphysical reality in which data informs, shapes, and makes up the built environment through vast interconnected systems and networks that enable natural, human, and technological processes to be rendered into electronic information that we call *data*. Unchecked, these systems and networks that permeate the postdigital world will result in systemic risks and collective harms that threaten the wellbeing of individuals, quality of relationships, sustainability of institutions, and even survival of democracies. In this brave new world, we must take a systemic approach that goes beyond data.

But what would it mean to go beyond data? There is a path forward, but it requires a hard reboot—a paradigmatic shift in the way that we think about and approach questions currently framed as those of data governance. We need a new and expanded main frame that reflects the new and expanded role of data in our lives and world at large—a role so expansive as to become an almost meaningless framework for technology governance.

In the previous chapters, I explored how powerful technology companies have distorted and diluted once-powerful notions of privacy and data protection in ways that further entrench and expand the considerable power and control they already exert over our individual and collective realities, and how the failure to impose limits on that power gives us a false sense of safety and security, while running the risk that privacy and data protection become the handmaidens of corporate surveillance and control.

The remainder of this book is devoted to avoiding these outcomes by imagining a path forward—one that goes beyond data to define our relationship to the technologies that mediate our lived experience. This chapter describes how the brave new postdigital, cyberphysical world that we are coming to inhabit upends our conventional legal and epistemological frameworks for data-centric technology governance, as illustrated by a host of technological advances. Chapter 6 explains why going beyond data actually requires us to begin *before* data, by imposing limits on datafication and its enablers, including meaningful limits on private power. And finally, chapter 7 takes us back to the future, returning to the human rights origins of data protection and privacy to refocus the technology governance conversation on people rather than on data.

Emotion Detection and Affect Recognition Technologies

In spring 2021, a coalition of musicians and human rights organizations from around the world published an impassioned letter to Spotify, urging the Sweden-based music streaming company to abandon any plans to use, license, sell, or monetize a controversial speech recognition technology it patented in 2018.[2] According to the patent, the technology would utilize "always-on" speech recognition and background noise detection tools to infer whether someone was listening to music alone, in a car, or in a group, and recommend tracks based on their mood, gender, age, accent, and surroundings.[3] Members of the coalition raised concerns about privacy, data security, discrimination, and the invasiveness of technologies that seek to infer and manipulate emotional states and behavior, noting that "monitoring emotional state, and making recommendations based on it, puts the entity that deploys the tech in a dangerous position of power in relation to a user."[4]

Although Spotify ultimately promised not to deploy the patented technology, the incident demonstrates a rapidly growing global market for so-called *emotion detection* or *affect recognition technologies*—a market that is expected to be worth more than US$37 billion by the year 2026.[5] Such technologies deploy machine learning along with other AI tools and techniques in an attempt to observe, infer, identify, and categorize an individual's personality traits as well as internal psychological and emotional states, such as anger, fear, surprise, happiness, and more, by sensing and collecting biometric inputs like facial expressions, voice quality or vocal tone, physical movements such as gait, typing or scrolling patterns or habits, and eye movements, and physiological markers such as heart rate, perspiration, body temperature, or blood pressure, among others.[6] Vehicle manufacturers are also widely employing affect recognition technologies to purportedly detect emotions,

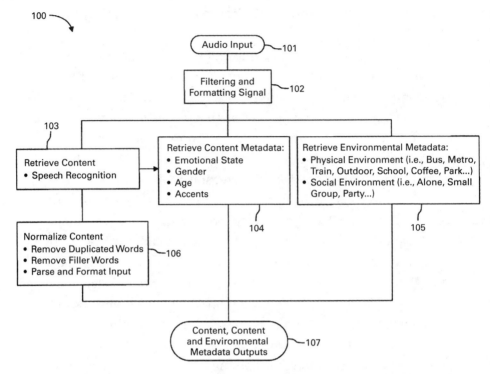

Spotify patent application for emotion-recognition-based song recommendations. *Source:* US Patent and Trademark Office via BBC (https://www.bbc.com/news/enter tainment-arts-55839655).

levels of attentiveness, distraction, or exhaustion, and other psychological and physiological states of drivers.[7]

While emotion or affect recognition technologies are being tested for music recommendations, driver safety systems, and other seemingly benign purposes, they are being explored for more consequential objectives too, such as to prevent or detect inauthentic or unauthorized behavior or criminality. For example, the use of facial recognition combined with affect recognition technologies for loss prevention in retail stores, fraud detection and prevention in financial services, exam proctoring and cheating detection in remote educational settings, and productivity monitoring in remote employment contexts, among other settings, is surging in popularity, in part accelerated by the shift to remote life during the COVID-19 pandemic. In China, emotion recognition technologies are being used in an attempt to detect whether students are attentive or happy in the classroom as well as to purportedly detect aggression, nervousness, and stress levels as part of crime prediction systems for customs and law enforcement purposes, in the hopes that these tools will help prevent or deter illegal acts like terrorism and smuggling.[8]

Neurotechnologies and Neuromarketing

Another new class of technologies is emerging that delves even deeper into our internal experience and personal boundaries. So-called *neurotechnologies* seek to integrate computers into human brains and nervous systems through neural interfaces that can communicate with the brain, central nervous system, peripheral nervous system, or autonomic nervous system, through both invasive and noninvasive means. Invasive means involve surgically implanting electrodes into a human brain to transmit neurological data to external computers, while noninvasive means may involve the transmission of brain signals through helmets and other wearable hardware devices.[9]

Categories of neurotechnologies include the *neuromodulation* technologies used to stimulate the nervous system, *neuroprostheses* used to control cognitive and other brain functions, and perhaps most widely known, *brain-machine* or *brain-computer interfaces* (BCIs). These technologies can "read" the brain by observing, recording, and interpreting brain activity as well as "write" to the brain by manipulating neural activity and function in specific regions of the brain to affect or alter their function.

The market for neurotechnologies is expected to reach US$19 billion by 2026 as they have a potentially wide array of applications, notably for medical interventions to treat mental, physical, cognitive, and neurological diseases, such as Alzheimer's, schizophrenia, and strokes.[10] For example, deep brain stimulation, which passes electric currents through regions of the brain to suppress neural activity, has been an approved treatment by the Food and Drug Administration for Parkinson's patients since as early as 1997.[11] More recently, in 2017, the potential of neurotechnologies for healing brain impairments was powerfully displayed when Rodrigo Hübner Mendes became the first quadriplegic person to pilot a Formula One car using the power of his thoughts alone.[12]

Neurotechnologies also have an array of commercial applications, particularly for mind-controlled consumer devices. For example, Facebook acquired CTRL-Labs, a New York–based neural interface, brain-computing start-up in 2019 to help its *augmented reality* (AR) arm, Facebook Reality Labs, develop a new AR wristband that uses electromyography to translate neural signals into movements and actions.[13] While not quite at the level of mind control, another New York–based BCI start-up has already obtained approval by the Food and Drug Administration for human clinical trials to test an implantable device designed to help paralyzed individuals control digital devices like computer cursors with their thoughts.[14] In fact, as of 2020, the private sector was outpacing federal funding for the development of new neurotechnologies.[15]

The potential for and interest in the commercial use of neurotechnologies for the purposes of *neuromarketing* is rapidly on the rise too. Through a combination of brain sensing, imaging, and scanning technologies, such as functional magnetic resonance imaging and electroencephalograms, as well as physiological tracking to measure eye movements, facial analysis tools, and other proxies for neural activity, marketers are exploring ways to leverage neuromarketing technologies to offer and adjust products and services, set prices, improve ads, and detect and influence consumer preferences and decisions. In the future, companies may even seek to create market segments based on individuals with similar neurological characteristics and proclivities, or adjust the lighting, temperatures, smells, and other sensory features in the physical environment to influence consumer propensities, even while sleeping.[16]

The Internet of Things and Bodies

Already ubiquitous, digitally embedded material devices are rapidly proliferating as the internet makes its way into everything through the IoT, sensors, and smart devices, increasingly implanting itself into our offices, homes, cities, and even brains and bodies. In fact, it is expected that there will be more than thirty billion IoT devices, more than four for every human on the planet, by the year 2025.[17] While digital tools and technologies are already widely deployed to operate as well as monitor a variety of infrastructure and activities in cities, municipalities, and industries around the world, the pervasiveness of sensors and IoT, coupled with advances in AI, AR and *extended reality* (XR), and 5G (and even 6G) wireless connectivity, will transform formerly digital environments into sentient ones, featuring complex networks of connected systems that continuously monitor and self-regulate their activities.

Just as IoT has transformed the external environment around us, a rapidly growing *Internet of Bodies* (IoB) is also emerging through networks of medical and biometric devices that attach to, or are inside of, our bodies and connected to the internet. While familiar examples include fitness trackers, smart watches, or other wearable devices, new and emerging IoB devices include "smart" contact lenses that can "zoom" in on objects or overlay visual displays, Bluetooth-enabled "smart" pills that can monitor as well as regulate the release and uptake of certain medications in the body, Wi-Fi-enabled pacemakers, and a host of other tools that can manipulate our biological, neurological, physiological, and other physical processes.[18] While many individuals also use these devices to self-monitor or even "biohack" their personal health, they are increasingly leveraged by third parties such as marketers or health insurance companies, which may use these devices to determine the scope and cost of insurance coverage, as one example.[19]

Beyond the familiar GUIs of computers, cell phones, and tablets, new computing interfaces are emerging for IoT and IoB, including BCIs, direct neural interfaces, and other human-computer interfaces that connect humans and machines in novel ways. Combined with IoB and neurotechnologies, these interfaces may eventually result in built environments in which humans, computers, and other objects are increasingly networked and connected. Moreover, new interfaces and display technologies, such as flexible screens or holograms, and increasingly sophisticated gestural and haptic interfaces will enable more lifelike multisensory experiences wherein the limits of computers are harder to perceive, rapidly eroding former distinctions between *online* and *offline* environments.[20] While these changes are still a way off from becoming mainstream, it would be prudent for legal and regulatory frameworks to anticipate and adopt a more sustainable approach in the face of them.

"Metaversal" Technologies

Further eroding the boundaries between the physical and digital worlds are a series of technologies designed to enhance our physical senses or foster immersive experiences with computer-generated components. They include VR technologies, which use headsets, controllers, and other hardware components to create fully immersive, computer-generated 3D content and experiences; AR technologies, which are focused on the physical world, but simply project or overlay digital elements onto it to alter or enhance an individual's perception of their surroundings or environment (a familiar example is the game *Pokémon Go*); and *mixed reality* (MR) technologies, which use advanced sensing and imaging technologies to combine physical and digital elements, resulting in an immersive experience in the physical world. VR, AR, and MR technologies are all instances of XR technologies, sometimes also referred to as the *metaverse* or what I deem to be *metaversal technologies*.

Once the stuff of science fiction, XR is quickly being rolled out in a variety of commercial and industrial settings. While gaming is currently the most popular and familiar application, XR is also being utilized in retail, healthcare, education, military and defense contexts, television and film production, travel, real estate, and sports, among other applications. For example, retailers and marketers are exploring applications that would allow consumers to virtually "try on" clothing or accessories, test out cosmetics on their faces, stage furniture in their living rooms, create virtual "pop-up" stores coupled with consumer apps, advertise in real time through AR-enhanced environments such as through 3D product placements, and more.[21] In the educational context, researchers are exploring whether XR might help facilitate learning in students with special needs.[22] Google, meanwhile, offers hundreds of virtual field trips known as "Expeditions" for students.[23] These technologies are being widely used to train employees and workers across industries too, including in the military, medical schools, and hospitals.[24] In late 2021, in the midst of the global pandemic, Facebook announced its plans to become a metaverse company, rebranding itself as Meta.[25]

As computing power and resources become cheaper and more readily available, including as 5G (and even 6G) wireless networks are deployed, XR will rapidly proliferate, with the global XR market projected to be worth nearly US$400 billion by 2025.[26] XR headsets along with other wearable and haptic devices may also incorporate BCIs, sensors, and emotion detection and recognition technologies in attempts to alter or adjust augmented or virtual experiences

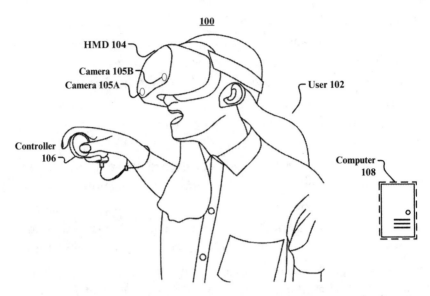

Facebook Technologies, LLC, patent application for "Systems, Methods, and Media for Automatically Triggering Real-time Visualization of Physical Environment in Artificial Reality." *Source*: US Patent and Trademark Office (https://pdfpiw.uspto.gov /.piw?PageNum=0&docid=11200745).

based on inferred or detected thoughts, moods, and emotions. In this way, immersive experiences might become responsive ones too, opening up myriad possibilities for personalization (and in turn, discrimination, as further explored in chapter 7). As with IoT and IoB, advances in XR will further integrate digital components into our physical and sensory experiences, simultaneously making these technologies more invisible and more influential.

"Phygital" Identity and Machine-Readable Humans

Even as the digital realm becomes more invisible, human beings are becoming more machine-readable through the proliferation of biometric-enabled digital identity tools and technologies. Already big business before the COVID-19 pandemic, the proliferation and adoption of digital identity tools and technologies for *identity and access management* (IAM) was further accelerated by the shift to remote life during the global public health emergency.[27]

Even beyond the use of IAM tools for accessing goods and services remotely or online, digital identity solutions are increasingly penetrating the physical world. For example, pandemic-induced germaphobia accelerated the adoption of *touchless* or *contactless* digital payments in lieu of cash or other alternatives, with uptake rising by nearly 15 percent in a matter of months, even as scientists emphasized that the risk of viral transmission through surfaces was extremely limited.[28] At the same time, the drive to manage the spread of the virus led to a proliferation of contact tracing or exposure notification apps, and later in the pandemic, digital proof-of-vaccination certificates and apps, as discussed in chapter 4. These apps quickly became necessary for international travel, access to certain retail and commercial experiences and venues, entry at workplaces and educational institutions, and more.[29] In these ways, the pandemic swiftly normalized the use as well as presentment of digital identity credentials and biometrics in the physical world—a phenomenon I refer to as *phygital identity*—including in contexts and settings where not previously necessary or required.[30]

Increasingly, these digital and phygital identity tools and technologies incorporate an array of biometrics, including physical biometrics such as facial prints or thumbprints, retinal or iris scans, and hand or palm vein recognition as well as behavioral biometrics like typing or scrolling habits, keystrokes, mouse movements, and other micromovements, and vocal tone and speech patterns, among others. Whereas physical biometrics require a single snapshot of a static physical trait, behavioral biometrics are established by observing and analyzing patterns of an individual's behavior over time. Biometric techniques are constantly evolving both in quantitative and qualitative terms, with some researchers even proposing the use of

BCIs and other neurotechnologies for biometric verification based on thought patterns and brain waves.[31]

AI and machine learning tools are also frequently used to process biometrics for IAM. For example, remote, AI-powered identity verification and authentication through the use of biometrics such as facial prints allow individuals to prove their identity by providing an image of their identity documents (such as a driver's license or passport) along with a live picture or video of their face. Machine learning models are then used to determine the likelihood that those documents are authentic (by extracting data from the document, and attempting to detect any digital or other manipulations of the photo), and conduct a facial similarity check to determine whether the facial image on the document matches the face in the selfie or video of the individual presenting it.[32] AI and ML tools and algorithms are also used to process and recognize patterns in behavioral biometrics-based systems.[33]

"Smart" Cities versus "Public" Spaces

Just as we are becoming more machine readable as humans, our built environments are becoming more saturated with sensors and machines to "read" us, including through the growth of smart cities. The OECD defines *smart cities* as "initiatives that use digital innovation to make urban service delivery more efficient and thereby increase the overall competitiveness of a community," while acknowledging that definitions vary widely across OECD countries and institutions. Japan, for instance, defines a *smart city* as "a sustainable city or region incorporating ICT and other new technologies to solve various challenges it faces and manages itself (planning, development, management and operation) for overall optimization."[34]

In general, smart cities are characterized by the incorporation of digital or ICT technologies for the delivery of municipal or public services for various ends, including economic competitiveness, environmental sustainability, and optimization of resources. Moreover, as big data processes, sensors, and connected technologies are increasingly deployed in urban areas, "cities themselves are creating data on us, sharing it, and using it to provide us with services, track us and communicate with us."[35] As scholar Ben Green observes in *The Smart Enough City*, "Embedding sensors, cameras, software, and an internet connection in everyday objects from streetlights to trashcans—creating what is known as the 'Internet of Things'—makes it possible to collect remarkably precise data about what is happening in a city."[36]

Smart cities are big business and growing bigger every day due to advances in IoT, extended 5G (and even 6G) access, and the declining cost and increasing availability of other digital tools and technologies. According to some market researchers, the size of the global smart city industry will double from nearly US$410.8 billion in 2020 to US$820.7 billion by 2025.[37] According to some studies, there is evidence that the global COVID-19 pandemic has further accelerated the rise of smart cities around the world too.[38]

Increasingly smart cities also involve public-private partnerships through which municipal governments procure technology from private companies in order to offer various services to their residents. As Green notes, "For companies, partnerships with cities present a rare and incredibly valuable opportunity to place data-gathering sensors throughout public spaces." But he further points out that the risks go far beyond data collection to actually transferring or shifting democratic decision-making power away from the public eye to private companies along with their proprietary tools and processes. For example, even as cities increasingly use algorithms for everything from policing to education, social services, and fire prevention, "municipal algorithms are concealed because they are developed and owned by private companies with a financial interest in secrecy."[39] This private ownership and control over the technical tools and processes that make cities run is changing the nature of *public* spaces in the cyberphysical world.

The public used to be a place of relative anonymity—where an individual could be one of many faces in the crowd. In this way, the public actually provided a similar zone of protection envisaged in traditional notions of privacy. But as a result of the widespread and growing deployment of privately owned and operated technologies in parks, city streets, and other common spaces, the emerging cyberphysical world is changing and challenging the notion of *public* spaces. In particular, generalized facial recognition technologies tied to real-world identities and the increasing pervasiveness of biometric-based digital identity solutions (including the use of advanced physical and behavioral biometrics), in combination with new IoT and IoB networks, threaten the notion of anonymity, even as they evade laws that are conditioned on the identifiability of individuals. Moreover, the private ownership and control of these digital identity infrastructures introduces commercial incentives and profit motives that conflict with core democratic values such as fairness, transparency, and accountability.

Data and the Cyberphysical World

As the technologies surveyed above demonstrate, in the emerging cyberphysical world, data is no longer confined to clearly discernible databases with limited purposes and plainly identifiable boundaries. Since at least the dawn of the second generation of the web or web 2.0, with its interactive nature, user-generated content, and large centralized platform intermediaries, the boundaries around data have grown ever harder to identify or define. These boundaries are only continuing to blur as the internet evolves from its largely web-based client-server architecture with information communicated through traditional GUI-based screens, into more distributed, decentralized, and peer-to-peer-style networks with new user interfaces that embed emotion recognition, neurotechnologies, and metaversal features that increasingly connect the experience of being human to our digital infrastructure.

As Laura DeNardis argues in *The Internet in Everything*, the transformation of the internet from ICT to a control network embedded directly into the physical world for operating systems and devices across every sector and industry, is a potentially more consequential shift than even the industrial revolution or the information age before it.[40] A world with the internet in everything is a world in which there is no longer any separation between the *physical* and *digital*, or between what is *online* and *offline*. It represents a structural transformation with considerable technical, commercial, political, and social consequences, disrupting global internet governance as we know it. To have any hope of effective governance in this brave new world, we must abandon our conventional database thinking and narrow conception of data as living within the domain of ICTs, as it did when the field of data protection first emerged, and instead embrace this new cyberphysical policy moment.

With the internet in everything, data is everywhere and nowhere, both ambient and native, forming a vast interconnected system of networks that transcend geographic borders and are not limited to ICT infrastructure. Instead, this infrastructure forms the de facto fourth estate, the public square, money and currency, critical infrastructure, and increasingly, the building blocks of democratic and autocratic institutions alike. For many of us, these technologies will also become the source, or at least a material part of, our livelihoods, education, relationships, and even personal identity as digital technologies gradually penetrate deeper into our psyches.

Moreover, as Mireille Hildebrandt contends in *Smart Technologies and the End(s) of Law*, we have moved from an information society to a data-driven one in which big data processes extend our human consciousness through a kind of *digital unconscious* that will "increasingly turn human agency itself into a new hybrid that is partly data-driven."[41] Legal scholar Julie Cohen further likens this digital unconscious to the limbic part of the human brain, in the sense that it is primitive, precognitive or mindless, impulsive, and highly vulnerable to algorithmic activation and manipulation.[42] Despite being largely invisible and inaccessible to us, this digital unconscious has significant implications for our actions and behaviors. As the Institute of Electrical and Electronics Engineers cautions, "Even as technologies fade into the background of our lives, they still play a pervasive role."[43]

As the digital fuses with the physical, data increasingly becomes the built environment around us, and creates a space that we collectively inhabit and cannot individually escape. Just as we long ago surpassed the point where we can realistically implement a push notification providing notice and seeking to obtain specific consent for every action requiring our data, it is time we acknowledge that no individual acting alone has any agency over this new cyberphysical reality, despite the presumption of individual control baked into existing legal frameworks. As Shoshana Zuboff puts it in *The Age of Surveillance Capitalism*, "Individuals each wrestling with the myriad complexities of their own data protection will be no match for surveillance capitalism's staggering asymmetries of knowledge and power. . . . [T]he individual alone cannot bear the burden of this fight at the new frontier of power."[44] Such asymmetries are further exacerbated by the nature of new technologies and increasing complexity of the postdigital, cyberphysical world that is emerging.

In the complexity of a fully interconnected, cyberphysical world, it is nearly impossible to predict in advance where data will travel, or what certain data points might reveal or enable down the line, particularly as AI, machine learning, and other computational technologies allow for new manipulations of data. As such, our new and expanded frame must also transcend other enduring but false dichotomies, such as *personal* or *non-personal* data, or *sensitive* versus *non-sensitive* data—determinations that cannot be made at the time of the data's origination. We must close the vast and dangerous divide between technologists and private interests that propagate a view of *privacy* as a technical, mathematical exercise in approaching anonymity (or at least reducing identifiability), on the one hand, and law and policy experts who understand *privacy* as a much broader concept necessary to protect the rights and interests of people in practice—a divide on heightened display as companies seek to weaponize privacy-enhancing technologies to further cement their power, influence, and profits (as explored in chapter 4).

When the digital becomes the built environment, the job of what we typically refer to as *data governance* is to make it safe, habitable, and sustainable. Because we share this environment, we must go beyond the limited notions of individual privacy and data protection, and transcend the atomicity that has characterized our efforts at data governance to date. Until we abandon our hyperindividualism and start addressing the fundamentals of power, we are unlikely to realize any meaningful change, and will continue to erode the values and norms that once underpinned our ways of relating to ourselves as well as each other. If we fail to evolve our thinking and persist down our current path of atomicity, we may individually consent our way into the same kind of surveillance state emerging in authoritarian regions of the world, especially in light of qualitatively different emerging technologies.

Advances in emotion recognition and neurotechnologies, the growth of invasive IoT and IoB devices, AR/VR, biometric-enabled digital and phygital ID systems, and other emerging technologies examined in this chapter present a whole new array of technical, legal, ethical, and moral challenges that can overwhelm the imaginative limits of existing laws and norms. Particularly as components of the digital realm become harder to isolate or govern as individual tools or technologies, we must go beyond technocratic, data-focused governance at a microlevel to consider the nature of digital technologies as part of complex sociotechnical systems. This need for systemic governance also reveals the limits of existing legal frameworks for privacy and data protection.

The Limits of Existing Legal Frameworks in the Cyberphysical World

The ubiquity of technologies that observe, track, and monitor our actions, movements, and other outward behaviors, such as location-based tracking technologies, already enable widespread surveillance by public and private actors alike, and can have a substantial chilling effect on speech, expression, and the exercise of civil and political rights, like the right to assemble or join a political protest. For example, cell phone location data can be used to track and monitor political protesters, as was the case with Black Lives Matter demonstrators across US cities in the wake of George Floyd's murder in Minneapolis in 2020.[45] But new and advanced technologies, including emotion recognition and neurotechnologies, threaten to go much further by attempting to infer and datafy our internal states and inner experiences of ourselves—and we have exceedingly limited protection from the present risks and potential harms of these technologies under existing legal frameworks.

Traditional conceptions of privacy, which long predate computing technologies, or any modern notions of data protection or data privacy, conceived of an almost physical space or boundary around the individual, designed to protect and promote the individual's internal or inner life, autonomy, and dignity. This physical and material conceptualization of privacy is also closely connected to the notion of *bodily integrity*, or the right of a person to participate in and make decisions about their own body, which underlies several other fundamental rights in the international human rights framework, including the security of the person as well as freedom from torture and cruel, inhuman, and degrading treatment, among others.[46] Near-universal agreement about the importance of this kind of boundary-based privacy, initially vis-à-vis the state or government, led to widespread political consensus codified through international human rights law.

But conventional privacy frameworks are increasingly challenged by their overly narrow conception of these physical boundaries, usually consisting of zones within our private residences or among our families, or with respect to the contents of our private correspondence, and only to a lesser extent, our physical or bodily integrity. Moreover, in many cases, as with the Fourth Amendment of the US Constitution, this kind of bounded privacy typically only protects us from interference by the government or other state actors—a highly limited notion in a postdigital world where much of our critical infrastructure is owned and operated by private entities, and where private technologies are also increasingly deployed in traditionally public spaces or settings, including in so-called smart cities.

The few privacy laws that exist in relation to private parties are arguably even more limited in nature. For example, US common law recognizes certain invasions of privacy by private entities as torts, including intrusion into seclusion, appropriation of likeness or identity, public disclosure of private facts, and portrayal in a false light.[47] Often, however, these torts also involve some kind of intrusion into a physical or delineable *private* space of an individual, and it is as yet unclear whether virtual activities can lead to litigable tort claims, with some prominent legal scholars deeming it unlikely. For instance, the potential liability of XR manufacturers, retailers, and other providers is ill-defined, particularly in the face of complex and diffuse supply chains along with complicated and layered interactions between technology hardware and software, user behavior, and real-world elements and considerations as well as novel jurisdictional questions raised by *where* experiences can be said to occur in XR settings.[48]

Equally limited are existing data protection frameworks that rely on an obsolete view of the digital world—a view that does not reflect the true nature of data in the cyberphysical, sentient environment that is rapidly emerging. Most data protection and privacy laws in place today presume the existence of a relationship between a party collecting data and a party whose data is being collected, even if it is an indirect one via third parties. As such, they assume that there is an opportunity, or at least a possibility, for the effective realization of core principles like transparency and accountability through various information and notices, processes, and procedures with respect to data collection and processing (even if these obligations have to flow down from one entity to another contractually). Furthermore, modern data protection frameworks focus exclusively on the processing of *personal data* or *personal information*, and, as a result, only protect us when we are identified or identifiable as a specific individual (and only at a given point in time). They also tend to presume some degree of distance or severability of data from an individual and their lived experience, despite the increasing commingling of the two as we become what some have termed *data bodies*.[49]

But data in a postdigital, cyberphysical, sentient world is anything that is observed, collected, inferred, created, and otherwise absorbed by sensors and digital infrastructure, including when it is attached to or embedded in human beings themselves—namely everything. In this way, digital infrastructure becomes gradually more invisible and insidious, while data collection becomes more passive and automatic and increasingly achieved through nontraditional user interfaces beyond smartphones and computer screens. The cyberphysical world also collapses the time and space required for implementing traditional pillars of data governance, such as notice and choice or obtaining affirmative consent, especially as presently conceived. Moreover, individuals become less aware of the entities rendering and harvesting data or inferences about them, especially as AI and machine learning tools and technologies proliferate. As a result, the relationships that underpin traditional data protection frameworks quickly break down, undermining the existing mechanisms for fairness, transparency, and accountability on which these laws typically depend.

Despite the growing complexity and opacity of the postdigital world, individuals are actually growing more identifiable through the proliferation of biometric-based digital identity–related tools and technologies, including ones that rely on or exploit the limitations of existing data protection frameworks. But digital technologies can also increasingly shape the attitudes and alter the behaviors of individuals and groups without directly identifying them. A growing array of technologies, including generalized biometric surveillance tools—such as facial recognition, emotion detection, and affect recognition technologies, behavioral monitoring and pattern recognition technologies, and neurotechnologies—can identify traits and other qualities about people without identifying them as specific individuals. In fact, these technologies are sometimes also referred to as *soft biometrics* because they can identify or characterize bodily traits and characteristics without necessarily identifying a person by a commercial or legal identity in the process.[50] Furthermore, big data and cyberphysical processes increasingly observe, collect, infer, and otherwise harvest the information of multiple individuals in the aggregate.

Even before the GDPR became law, the European Data Protection Supervisor anticipated the shortcomings of a governance framework that hinges on individual identifiability, observing that "'big data' should be considered personal even where anonymization techniques have been applied: it is becoming ever easier to infer a person's identity by combining allegedly 'anonymous' data with other datasets including publicly available information for example on social media."[51] Given the GDPR's influence in shaping subsequent legal frameworks, similar shortcomings have been replicated around the world. For example, many data protection and privacy laws, deem aggregated, anonymized, or deidentified information to fall outside the scope of what constitutes personal data or personal information and therefore exempt from the law's requirements.[52]

Even where they are not identifiable, increasingly advanced AI tools, machine learning technologies, and algorithms enable consequential inferences about individuals and groups from personal data, as well as non-personal, nonidentifiable, or aggregated anonymized data.[53] As such, much of the data observed, collected, inferred, and otherwise absorbed by sensors and digital infrastructure, particularly when processed via AI or machine learning tools, may not be *personal data* as defined by existing data protection frameworks, particularly at the point at which it is initially harvested. As Oxford researchers Sandra Wachter and Brent Mittelstadt argue, "Data protection law is meant to protect people's privacy, identity, reputation, and autonomy, but it is currently failing to protect data subjects from the novel risks of inferential analytics [as] individuals are granted little control or oversight over how their personal data is used to draw inferences about them."[54]

In fact, at present, information observed or harvested in public spaces that does not identify or single out any specific individual, data that has been aggregated and anonymized or deidentified, and large swaths of inferential data points, remain largely outside the scope or protection of data protection laws or other personal data-based legal frameworks. And increasingly, technologically mediated processes and activities will evade existing laws and regulations that hinge on the notion of *personal data* or *identifiability*, remaining almost entirely unregulated insofar as they do not identify or single out specific individuals.[55] Moreover, as we saw in chapter 4, industry is continually deploying a wider array of PETs and other technical tools and methods to anonymize, pseudonymize, deidentify, and encrypt data in ways that can take it outside the scope of existing legal protections.

Taken together, these trends deepen the asymmetries of power between individuals and private corporations that own and control these technologies. In light of the growing gap between emerging technological realities and our existing legal frameworks, it is time that we expand our focus beyond limited or fixed notions of personal data and individual identifiability. As one AI scholar observes, "Questions of ethics, emotion capture and making bodies passively machine-readable by emotional AI is not contingent upon personal identification, but human dignity, choice and decisions about what kinds of environments we want to live in."[56] But the same concerns extend well beyond emotion recognition technologies. As technocratic views of digital governance based on personal data are meeting their limits in the postdigital, cyberphysical world, we must forge a new path that goes beyond data by addressing the underlying enablers of datafication at the hands of private power. That is the subject of the next chapter.

6

Against the Datafication of Life

Just as the emergence of computers and digital databases in the twentieth century threatened traditional notions of privacy and gave rise to the modern concept of data protection, new and advanced technologies that purport or attempt to observe and analyze our physiological, psychological, cognitive, and emotional states by penetrating deeper and deeper into our personal boundaries undermine existing data protection and privacy frameworks—particularly ones that are focused on imposing limits on the use, security, or management of personal data. Combined with the qualitatively different role that data plays in a postdigital, cyberphysical world, in which data comprises the built environment, and the increasing machine readability of humans through AI, machine learning, and other computational methods, we desperately need a new approach.

Our obsession with data, especially personal data, in the face of these emerging technologies, and the evolving relationship between humanity and digital technologies in a postdigital world, obscures what is really at stake in the new cyberphysical reality—namely the integrity of the self that enables individual autonomy, the formation of social and political relationships, and the foundations for democratic institutions and governance. It is high time that we look beyond data to discern the signal in the noise and reestablish this personal integrity. One potentially powerful approach is to actually begin *before* data enters the equation by ending the exceptional treatment of certain entities as "technology companies," and challenging the narratives and processes that enable them to render human life and experience into digital data in the first place. That is the subject of this chapter.

The Exceptional Treatment of "Tech Companies"

As cars soared in popularity in the twentieth century, so too did vehicular fatalities, with the rate of automobile-related deaths doubling between 1920 and 1960.[1] Even as nearly 80 percent of US households had at least one vehicle in 1960, the US automobile industry remained almost entirely unregulated through the mid-1960s.[2] It was not until Harvard-educated lawyer Ralph Nader published the groundbreaking book *Unsafe at Any Speed: The Designed-In Dangers of the American Automobile* in 1965, accusing automobile manufacturers of designing for style and profit at the expense of consumer safety, that Congress acted to pass the National Traffic and Motor Vehicle Safety Act of 1966.[3] The act established the National Highway Safety Bureau, which later became the National Highway Traffic Safety Administration, and introduced the first federal safety standards for all US-manufactured automobiles, including mandatory seat belt installation in all passenger vehicles.

Today it is hard to imagine leaving automobiles unregulated. But throughout history, countless new industries, such as cars, tobacco, and chemicals as well as many predigital technologies, have enjoyed periods of relative lawlessness and exceptional treatment. More recently, a similar phenomenon has unfolded with respect to the so-called *technology sector*, which is typically defined to include companies that design, develop, or support computer operating systems and software applications; companies engaged in the manufacturing of hardware equipment, data storage products, networking products, semiconductors, and components; and companies that provide technology-related consulting services.[4] Increasingly, though, as more and more companies have software-based offerings and applications, the boundaries of this sector are becoming harder to discern, even as *tech* has become a kind of free pass to escape regulation or governance.

The infiltration of traditional sectors and industries by digital tools and technologies over the last two decades has spawned a flurry of *-tech* neologisms, from *fintech* in finance to *edtech* in education, *healthtech* in healthcare, *cleantech* in environmental technologies, *insuretech* in insurance, *legaltech* in legal services, and so on. And while financial services companies are not exempt from regulations despite their heavy reliance on new and advanced technologies, nor are medical professionals released from liability based on their use of cutting-edge, digital surgical or medical tools, the *-tech* characterization has frequently freed technology firms from having to meet the same requirements as their traditional counterparts without this suffix. For example, while invasive BCIs that require surgical implantation are typically regulated as medical devices, noninvasive BCIs are considered consumer technologies and are largely unregulated, apart from generally applicable consumer protection regulations that are ill-equipped for the kinds of novel risks and harms arising from such neurotechnologies.

Whereas these traditional industries and sectors are subject to a complex array of domain-specific laws and regulations intended to provide minimum safety and quality standards as well as protect individuals and society from undue risks and systemic harms, technology-based interventions into these domains often escape similar rules or regulations. Traditional banks, for instance, are subject to significant oversight and comprehensive regulatory frameworks, while peer-to-peer lending apps are not; similarly, medical devices are heavily regulated, while consumer wearables, such as health and fitness trackers, are not. This exceptional treatment of technology companies enables an increasing array of companies to evade all manner of laws and regulations. Coupled with the notion of *technological determinism*—the belief that social progress is driven by technological innovation, which in turn follows an "inevitable" course—many industry payers remain largely unconstrained by regulations or regulators afraid of quelling this innovation.[5]

At some point, however, the risks of a new technology or industry clearly begin to outweigh the benefits of such a hands-off approach, and regulation becomes necessary and appropriate. We are well past this point with respect to many digital technologies. By leaving these technologies and applications largely unregulated, we inadvertently introduce and accept unmitigated risks across all industries that these technologies touch—namely all industries. Lawmakers are slowly beginning to embrace the end of this special treatment, even as they maintain exceptional rhetoric and language. For example, the European Commission has repeated the mantra of "What is illegal offline is illegal online," including as it has introduced new rules and regulations for digital platforms.[6] This attitude is especially concerning as we are at a moment in time when virtually every company is a technology company, such that if we were to spare technology companies from any lawful limits on their activities, we would effectively engender lawlessness.

Moreover, because technology companies typically run on digital data, we frequently attempt to use data protection or data privacy frameworks to address or solve all manner of problems that such frameworks are unprepared to address, as if data-related governance mechanisms could somehow replace governance more generally. We may believe, say, that a robust data protection or privacy law could sufficiently mitigate the risks stemming from health-related consumer wearable technologies that are not supplied by regulated health providers or do not constitute medical devices under existing regulations.[7] Likewise, we may expect data privacy regulations to serve as adequate governance for retail trading apps or alternative lending platforms that algorithmically determine interest rates, even as these tools fall outside the scope of traditional financial regulations.[8] Without effective laws or regulations to govern the activities of data-driven technology companies, we tend to rely too much on data protection and privacy frameworks, expecting them to act as panaceas for our technology-related governance woes.

But not everything involving data or digital technologies is a question of data protection or even data governance, at least not exclusively. The frame is too narrow, and risks reducing questions of privacy and human rights more generally to technocratic questions about data. In other words, when everything is digital, there are effectively no longer *digital rights*, only *rights*. When everything is data, *data governance* becomes a matter of *governance*. When data is everything and everywhere, coursing through the built environment and mediating our relationship to reality, it loses the ability to anchor a society in governing this relationship between humans and technology. Instead, we require a better anchor or different starting point. We must begin building a new consensus around the norms that will govern this data-mediated relationship, including limits on the specific processes that result in data in the first place.

Datafication and Its Enablers

In *Big Data*, Kenneth Cukier and Viktor Mayer-Schönberger define *datafication* as the process of rendering previously unquantified aspects of the world into the numerically quantified format of digital data so that it can be tabulated and analyzed.[9] Whereas *digitization* (or *digitalization*) merely transforms previously analog content such as books or music into machine-readable digital content, datafication turns hitherto noninformational aspects of life into data that can be used to track, measure, surveil, predict, nudge, and otherwise analyze or influence human behavior at both an individual and collective level.

Cukier and Mayer-Schönberger argue that datafication actually transforms the nature of whatever is being datafied, turning it into new forms of value. In the context of capitalism, datafication involves the abstraction and extraction of insights from life to generate profit, enabling the commodification of previously uncommodified aspects of human experience.[10] Examples include Facebook datafying friendships and interests, Twitter datafying casual conversations and stray thoughts, or LinkedIn datafying professional networks of employees and job seekers, among others.[11] If these Web2 platforms sought to datafy *outward* expressions of our personality or relationships, Web3 or metaversal technologies seek to datafy everything, including our external and *internal* physiological, psychological, cognitive, and emotional states.

In addition to quantification, datafication both creates and is sustained by the illusion of *dematerialization*. In *Being Digital*, Nicholas Negroponte described the phenomenon of digitization as going from atoms to electronic data in the form of *bits*. According to Negroponte, bits move at the speed of light, and unlike atoms, do not obey the laws of general relativity with respect to matter, space, or time. Negroponte also argued that "the change from atoms to bits is irrevocable and unstoppable."[12] But as Dutch legal theorist Mireille Hildebrandt points out, "Bits and bytes are made of atoms, inscribed on silicon chips. However small, they are a matter of matter, and that matters."[13] In this way, digital data is still subject to the laws of time and space. Nevertheless, this vantage point of demateriality, of a realm outside the laws of nature, supports powerful and enduring myths around the inevitability of certain technological innovations along with the exceptional treatment of firms that introduce them.

Similarly, we can think of datafication as a way of taking things from the material world and appearing to turn them into digital, ethereal, and dematerialized forms, obscuring the concrete time, energy, materials, and other resources giving rise to the resultant data. As Kate Crawford notes in *Atlas of AI*, just as with terms like *cloud computing* that have an ethereal connotation, "*data* has become a bloodless word [that] disguises both its material origins and ends."[14] As with many technology-related metaphors, the mythology around the demateriality of data and processes of datafication support continued and growing extraction for profit, serving already powerful interests. Quantification, commodification, dematerialization, and mythologization are powerful and enduring enablers of datafication as well as the underlying process of rendition.[15]

In *The Age of Surveillance Capitalism*, Shoshana Zuboff uses the term *rendition* to describe the concrete operational practices and processes by which human experience is claimed as raw material for datafication. Through rendition, "intimate territories of the self, like personality and emotion, are claimed as observable behavior and coveted for their rich deposits of predictive surplus [and] the personal boundaries that shelter inner life are officially designated as bad for business by a new breed of mercenaries of the self, determined to parse and package inner life for the sake of surveillance revenues."[16] For Zuboff, it is the original sin of surveillance capitalism, without which the practice could not exist. In other words, rendition relentlessly seeks to erode any boundaries around the self, whether physical, mental, psychological, or emotional, for the sake of profit. The ongoing erosion of these boundaries through an array of new and advanced technologies that enable rendition threatens the autonomy of the individual and minimal integrity of the self that is foundational to privacy as well as numerous other fundamental rights under international human rights law.

Moreover, alongside threats to the individual, datafication exploits entire communities and societies. For scholars Nick Couldry and Ulises Mejias, datafication can be understood as a new colonial process whereby human life and social resources are appropriated for continuous data extraction, dispossessing some for the benefit and profit of Western (and increasingly, global) capitalist interests—a process they term *data colonialism*. Through this lens, datafication can be viewed as another form of extractivism and appropriation rooted in a long history of colonialism. The beneficiaries of data colonialism are predominantly large corporations that own and control the infrastructures that enable this extraction in the first place. This push for unfettered connection, datafication, and personalization by corporations is supported by "the myth that this is all inevitable and that today's infrastructures of connection and data extraction fulfill human beings' collective potential in some transcendent way."[17] A material example of this logic is the rhetoric employed by firms such as Meta and Google as they quite literally and physically encircle entire continents with undersea cables in pursuit of connection at all costs.[18]

As captured by the title of venture capitalist Marc Andreesen's 2011 article in the *Wall Street Journal*, "Software Is Eating the World," Silicon Valley has always had an insatiable appetite for rendition. But by going beyond physical and human resources, the shift to a data-driven economy has only intensified this drive. As Crawford observes, this emergent logic, or "belief that everything is data and there for the taking," has pervaded the technology sector, which in reality is now nearly every sector, thereby further extending the reach of this logic across private industry more generally.[19] Emotion recognition and neurotechnologies aimed at mining our internal states are prime illustrations of this phenomenon.

The Inadequacies of Data Protection

Rhetoric and mythologies aside, there is nothing inevitable or immaterial about datafication or rendition, especially with respect to our internal lives and lived experiences. Naming, identifying, and understanding these processes and phenomena can help us invoke their limits, and identify aspects of personality, community, and humanity that cannot or should not be quantified and rendered for neocolonial capital extraction through datafication. Rather, we can and should impose limits on datafication and rendition directly, starting with the underlying assumptions and processes that enable it, including the privately owned and operated infrastructures and processes that render human life and experience into digital data in the first instance. Regrettably, data protection is not up to the task.

Limits on datafication are not the same as familiar data protection principles found in existing laws or regulations. For instance, the GDPR provides that "personal data shall be collected for specified, explicit and legitimate purposes" (the *collection limitation* principle), "not further processed in a manner that is incompatible with those purposes" (the *purpose limitation* principle), and "adequate, relevant and limited to what is necessary in relation to the purposes for which they are processed" (the *data minimization* principle).[20] Similarly, the forthcoming California Privacy Rights and Enforcement Act combines these principles into a single requirement that "a business' collection, use, retention, and sharing of a consumer's personal information shall be reasonably necessary and proportionate to achieve the purposes for which the personal information was collected or processed, or for another disclosed purpose that is compatible with the context in which the personal information was collected, and not further processed in a manner that is incompatible with those purposes."[21]

As codified in existing laws, these principles are not enough to resist datafication in a postdigital, cyberphysical world for a variety of reasons, some of which I outlined in chapter 5. Nevertheless, it is important to revisit the inadequacies of data protection in the face of rapacious datafication in a postdigital world. Existing laws presume at least a modicum of time and space between a party collecting data and the party whose data is being collected, rather than the kind of passive or automatic data collection that is increasingly occurring as we move into a sentient world with the internet in everything. Some might argue that data protection laws such as the GDPR do, at least to a limited extent, account for passive or automatic data collection, and prohibit it without a legitimate interest or other purpose-limited justification. But such limitations do not even take effect or come into play until a data subject (or data subjects) are identified or identifiable, which is often not the case at this stage of passive data collection, as it would not yet be *personal data* collection, making it easier to skirt the spirit and letter of these laws.

Second, existing data protection frameworks presume some kind of visibility or relationship between parties on opposite sides of this passive or automatic data collection, such as between a business and its consumers (or a *data controller* and *data subject* in the case of the GDPR), with no appreciation for the complexity or obscurity of the parties that are observing, harvesting, and absorbing data en masse. Here, data protection and privacy practitioners and scholars might object that the notion of a *data processor* is intended to cover data collected by parties that may be unknown or obscure to those whose data is being collected. Yet the obligations of a data processor (or similar entity) are legal and organizational requirements that must "flow down" via a contract or other binding mechanism, as between that entity and a data controller (or similar entity) that determines the purposes and nature of collection and processing. This legal and procedural chain of custody is increasingly challenged, though, in the face of new types of legal and technical entities and organizational structures. In the case of AI and machine learning, for example, the entity akin to a data controller may obtain initial data sources from an open or common resource (such as a data set library) without any contractual relationship to that source as a processor (or equivalent entity).

But perhaps most importantly, as explored in chapter 5, these principles and the frameworks in which they are found continue to presume the existence of, and only apply to, data points that satisfy technical definitions of *personal data* or *personal information*. While it is true that most data, over time, and when combined with other data, easily satisfies the legal definition of *personal data* or *personal information*, there remains a sequencing problem in the way most existing data protection laws are designed. Specifically, they fail to account for the reality that an increasing array of new and advanced technologies sweep up hordes of data that would not meet these requirements at the time of their collection or processing, despite the risks to individuals, particularly with respect to data deemed to be aggregated, anonymized, or deidentified.[22] Coupled with the fact that lawmakers and policymakers are increasingly incentivized to find exceptions and carve outs from these definitions so as not to stifle innovation, the result is a substantial loophole in our existing paradigm for data-centric technology governance.

The postdigital, cyberphysical world is increasingly always on, sentient, observing, and capable of influencing or manipulating our individual and collective thoughts, feelings, or actions. Thus by the time something has been rendered into data, it may be too late to negotiate what that data represents, how it is coded or interpreted, how it is used or ingested into other systems or processes, or how it is being (or ultimately could be) wielded to make consequential decisions about people. Furthermore, the decision and capacity to render and datafy in the first place highlights steep power asymmetries, such as between the parties undertaking the rendering or datafication and the parties being rendered or datafied. In other words, by the time something has been datafied, it is often too late to negotiate on the grounds of power, inclusion, equity, or fairness. As Couldry and Mejias observe, "Automatic data collection poses a danger to autonomy . . . not because its actual uses are always harmful (indeed, some might be beneficial) but because the *possibility* of harmful use distorts the space in which individuals live and act."[23]

Effective governance in this context requires that we collectively prenegotiate new norms for the cyberphysical world, beginning with identifying and imposing limits on things that cannot or should not be turned into data at all. Going beyond data protection principles like data minimization, collection limitation, or purpose limitation, limits on datafication would challenge underlying claims to render or colonize domains of human experience and existence into data, metrics, analytics, and capital in the first place. They would invalidate and delegitimize industry's claims to certain domains of human life and experience. Critically, to preserve and protect fundamental rights, we need to ask what the permissible scope of datafication is in the first place. As a society (and specifically, as lawmakers and policymakers), we must negotiate, articulate, and seek to codify the boundaries of rendition and datafication by the owners and operators of digital tools, technologies, and infrastructures, including through natural and normative limits.

Natural Limits on Datafication

First, we should acknowledge the natural limits of datafication. Namely there are some things that simply cannot be rendered or datafied with any degree of accuracy, integrity, or reliability. Rather, attempting to datafy these domains merely results in proxy data as opposed to any underlying truth or objective observation. In fact, technologies of datafication are frequently riddled with well-documented limitations and shortcomings, and risk leading us to draw faulty or erroneous assumptions and inferences about our internal states or proclivities from our outward expressions and appearances. But even when they do not work, these technologies can actively cause disproportionate harm when they are perceived as or treated *as if* they were capable of rendering true or objective insights, which are then used to make or inform decisions with significant legal, economic, or political consequences. The natural limits on datafication are particularly prominent in the context of emotion or affect recognition technologies and neurotechnologies.

In that regard, there is no agreement among scientists that AI can even detect emotions or personality traits in the first place. In reality, what these technologies actually detect are nonverbal behaviors or cues, such as micro-expressions, motor movements, and certain other bodily movements. But many researchers have documented wide variance in how people communicate their emotional states across cultures and situations, and even among different individuals in the same situation. Studies have also demonstrated how the same combination of facial movements or expressions can express more than a single emotion at the same time. Moreover, these movements and behaviors are influenced by a combination of highly specific internal and external factors, including environmental factors such as light or noise levels, which are often not adequately addressed or accurately captured by machine learning models. Put simply, nonverbal behaviors associated with certain emotional or psychological states are known to be nonspecific, context sensitive, and highly variable across individuals and cultures, making automated emotion or affect recognition technologies highly unreliable.[24]

Yet even as they don't work, these technologies can pose serious risks to people. Indeed, some scholars liken emotion detection and recognition technologies to the discredited pseudosciences of phrenology and physiognomy of the late nineteenth and early twentieth centuries, which attempted to infer mental abilities from skull shapes or sizes, and character or personality from facial expressions or features.[25] Attempting to render or datafy these internal states, including by importing discredited theories of emotion into digital systems, can create the illusion of accuracy or certainty that

"Grades of Intelligence," in Samuel Wells, *New Physiognomy* (1868), an example of pseudoscientific classification justifying discrimination based on physical character-istics. The illustration was designed "to convey an idea of the different grades of development and intelligence as indicated in profile, size, as well as form." *Source:* Wikimedia (https://commons.wikimedia.org/wiki/File:Wells,_Physiognomy_(1868) _n.142.jpg).

data affords, and in turn, threaten the rights of individuals and groups alike.

Just as the history of using technology to make assessments about someone's character on the basis of physical or outward appearances is riddled with racial, gender, and other biases, modern emotion and affect recognition technologies can similarly reinforce racist and misogynistic hierarchies.[26] For instance, automated tools for interpreting emotional states from facial expressions have been shown to exhibit racial bias, consistently interpreting Black faces as having more negative emotions than white ones.[27] Researchers have also identified age and gender biases, including variable degrees of accuracy in depicting different types of emotions as between male or female faces as well as differences in accuracy depending on whether a machine learning model was trained on the faces of a single gender or multiple genders.[28]

Another example of a class of technologies riddled with natural limitations is neurotechnology, particularly tools that purport to decode neural activity to "read minds" or detect a person's intentions. Typically, these technologies rely on observing *neural correlates*—correlations between mental states, such as emotions, intentions, or perceptions, and electric activity or neural patterns in the brain. But the neural correlates of psychological and cognitive phenomena, including the neural circuitry for decision-making, are imprecise and poorly understood by science.[29] According to some scholars, "Neural prostheses may allow reading neural correlate fragments of mental states but not the whole mind on its global scale. The extent to which all the pieces of thoughts that can be decoded from neural recordings constitute whole thoughts thus remains unclear."[30]

Moreover, because neural activity does not perfectly correlate with mental or emotional states, it has to be processed, interpreted, and translated into data through the use of AI and machine learning algorithms before being "downloaded" or "read" through a BCI or another device. Often, these algorithms are complex, opaque, and privately owned, introducing sometimes unintelligible, unpredictable, and unaccountable processes between an individual's thoughts or feelings and the technology that is used to communicate or express them.[31] These challenges are further exacerbated by the use of predictive tools and technologies that automatically complete or correct outcomes; just consider how rudimentary existing autofill and autocorrect tools are for text messages or word processing applications, and then imagine the implications for using these technologies to complete or predict patterns of thought or expression.

But regardless of whether these technologies *can* actually read minds, they are at risk of being applied *as if* they do. Furthermore, they may be interpreted as accurate and objective, even where that is most certainly not the case. As with emotion and affect recognition technologies, neurotechnologies can pose serious risks to individuals, even when they do not perform as anticipated or described, when their outputs are used to make actionable determinations or inferences about individuals in a variety of contexts.[32] These risks, for instance, would be considerably heightened in the context of legal decisions or criminal justice applications where neurotechnologies may be used to infer mental states or motivations.[33] As such, recognizing the natural limits of these technologies is of critical importance in imposing limits on datafication.

In addition, when we start from the perspective of data, without challenging what has been subject to datafication, we obscure important political and moral questions that new technologies raise. As Sun-Ha Hong argues in *Technologies of Speculation*, datafication and quantification are actually social technologies. Specifically, he explains that "just as the pursuit of better knowledge through datafication entails a social shift in what counts as objectively true, the collective faith in the purity of data entails using the data to try to bypass important political and moral questions, to try to purify bodies through technological solutions." In doing so, we risk entrenching existing power structures, such as racial and gender dynamics, and perpetuating the status quo. In a world marked by complexity and uncertainty, and mounting political and ethical challenges posed by new technological interventions, datafication "seeks to become our groundless ground." Our collective belief in these *epistemic fantasies*, as Hong calls them, transforms what counts as truth and certainty.[34]

Recognizing the inherent limitations of some of the tools, techniques, and technologies of datafication or speculation is the first step in resisting these processes. Naming the natural limits of these technologies also buys us time to articulate normative limits for existing and future harms, in line with the *precautionary principle*, or idea that "when human activities may lead to morally unacceptable harm that is scientifically plausible but uncertain, actions shall be taken to avoid or diminish that harm."[35] For example, legal scholar Susie Alegre argues that technological developments that threaten to interfere with our freedom of thought fall within the scope of "morally unacceptable harm" and trigger the precautionary principle (the instructiveness of human rights in this regard is further explored in chapter 7).[36] By identifying the natural limitations of neurotechnologies today, we can begin to identify moral limits and establish normative constraints on their future uses.

Normative Limits on Datafication

Even where certain aspects of our lives and experiences can, as a practical matter, be rendered and datafied with any degree of accuracy, integrity, or reliability, whether now or in the future, there are still, as a matter of principle, some things that we simply should not allow to be subjected to these processes. Rather, we should prohibit their rendition and datafication in the first place. This is especially true of the domains of our inner life and experience, consisting of our unexpressed thoughts, feelings, inclinations, and emotions, as they are vital to personal identity, dignity, autonomy, and the integrity of the self—and in turn, these are essential components of a cohesive society. The basis for such normative prohibitions is rooted in both ethical and moral philosophy, including the moral limits of markets.

Whereas things like thoughts, feelings, and emotions were previously outside the scope of markets, their quantification through the processes of rendition and datafication brings them into the market, giving them economic value. Echoing philosopher Hannah Arendt's observations regarding the cycle of capital accumulation, by which more aspects of the social and natural world are subordinated to the market dynamic, Zuboff explains, "Industrial capitalism transformed nature's raw materials into commodities, and surveillance capitalism lays its claim to the stuff of human nature for a new commodity invention. Now it is human nature that is scraped, torn, and taken for another century's market project."[37] Or as digital media scholar Andrew McStay characterizes it, "A strata of humanity that was once systematically off-limits to commerce may be mined and datafied."[38]

Through this accelerating and ever-expanding market project of datafication, Couldry and Mejias caution that we are at risk of unlearning norms associated with autonomy and freedom for the self. As they provocatively ask, "Can we imagine installing an app or a chip that measured whether one was really in love with someone? Or an app that compared the depth of one's grief for a loved one against the grief of others for the same, or for a different, person? When exactly does our expanding submission to the self's datafication come up against something that we feel we must be protected from at all costs?"[39]

The datafication of previously non-data aspects of our lives as well as our inner selves should raise a moral and ethical discomfort that points to a deeper problem with industry's unrelenting appetite for datafication—namely the limitless commodification or financialization of human behavior and experience. Where everything can be turned into quantitative data for computation and analysis for value extraction, so too can everything be transformed into a new commodity for the market. Without limits to rendition and datafication, there are arguably no limits to markets in a post-digital society. And without such limits, it would be virtually impossible to prevent certain negative effects such as discrimination and inequality.

For moral philosopher Michael Sandel, commodification is a moral question as much as it is an economic or political one because it challenges us to identify what we value and how we value it. In this way, the ability to commodify human experience through datafication represents a political act by which market norms crowd out the nonmarket norms associated with that experience. As Sandel cautions, "Altruism, generosity, solidarity, and civic spirit are not like commodities that are depleted with use. They are more like muscles that develop and grow stronger with exercise. One of the defects of a market-driven society is that it lets these virtues languish."[40]

The datafication and, in turn, commodification of everything may also threaten core democratic values such as equity and inclusion. As Sandel asserts, "The more money can buy, the more affluence (or the lack of it) matters." He posits that "the commodification of everything has sharpened the sting of inequality by making money matter more," and "corrodes commonality" by causing us to lead increasingly separate and stratified lives on the basis of what we can afford.[41] Just as there are concerns about social media technologies contributing to echo chambers that exacerbate political polarization, we should consider how unlimited datafication threatens the common ground necessary for a functioning democracy.

The erosion of these values, and thus social and political common ground, are increasingly at risk in the face of existing but inadequate data protection frameworks that fail to set normative limits on datafication. As Couldry and Mejias observe about the limits of existing regulations such as the GDPR, "The GDPR changes the rules under which data colonialism operates but leaves unchallenged the commercial purposes for which data is collected."[42] Bearing in mind that the GDPR is presently considered the gold standard of data governance frameworks, this should be cause for alarm and a reaffirmation of why we must intervene even earlier in the process than existing data protection laws do.

Some scholars have called for the imposition of various normative limits on certain kinds of data markets or datafication activities. In her book *Privacy Is Power*, for example, Carissa Véliz posits that data is power, and argues that in order to rein in the surveillance economy, we actually need to ban the data economy outright. Specifically, Véliz calls for a ban on markets in personal data, contending that "personal data should not be sold, disclosed, transferred, or shared in any way for the purposes of profit or commercial advantage," along with outright bans on targeted behavioral advertising and data brokering.[43]

That data is power is only partly true. As scholar Michael Veale points out, "It's commonly said that in the digital world, data is power. This simple view might apply to a company collecting data through an app or a website, such as a supermarket, but doesn't faithfully capture the source of power of the firms controlling the hardware and software platforms these apps and websites run on. Using privacy technologies, such as 'federated' or 'edge' computing, Apple and Google can understand and intervene in the world, while truthfully saying they never saw anybody's personal data."[44] As I explored in chapter 4, there is much more to power than data in a postdigital, cyberphysical world. And, as I further examined in chapter 5, emerging technologies will increasingly wield power without (or before) implicating notions of *personal data*. As such, prohibiting the trade of personal data is inherently limited.

Although Véliz acknowledges that there are vulnerabilities in the way that existing laws and regulations rely on a narrow definition of *personal data*, she ultimately depends on these ontologies, including the flawed and slippery notions of *personal data* and *sensitive data*. For example, she argues that "the more sensitive the data, the stricter the ban and the steeper the penalty for breaking the law ought to be."[45] Moreover, she calls for the heightened application and enforcement of the data minimization and collection limitation principles to indirectly stop the trade in personal data, despite the limitations I have already highlighted with respect to these principles as applied to a postdigital, cyberphysical world.

In *The Age of Surveillance Capitalism*, Zuboff goes a step further, recommending that we outlaw markets in human behavioral futures entirely. As she explains, "As long as surveillance capitalism and its behavioral futures markets are allowed to thrive, ownership of the new means of behavioral modification eclipses ownership of the means of production as the fountainhead of capitalist wealth and power in the twenty-first century." According to Zuboff, "If new laws were to outlaw extraction operations, the surveillance model would implode."[46] In other words, we must focus on control over the *means of and infrastructure for* behavioral modification, over and above concentrating on control over *data*, including by prohibiting certain forms of rendition and datafication.

Increasingly, civil society and advocacy organizations are calling for outright bans, at least on some uses of these technologies. For example, advocacy group AI Now contends, "Given the contested scientific foundations of affect recognition technology . . . it should not be allowed to play a role in important decisions about human lives, such as who is interviewed or hired for a job, the price of insurance, patient pain assessments, or student performance in school . . . [and] governments should specifically prohibit use of affect recognition in high-stakes decision-making processes."[47] As another illustration, pressure from civil society advocates and academic researchers such as Joy Buolamwini led to Amazon, Microsoft, IBM, and other companies halting their development of facial recognition technologies and ending their sales of the technology to law enforcement, while several cities and municipalities enacted outright bans.[48] These are also clear examples of how natural limits must inform our normative limits. Further, they illustrate that regardless of how well personal data is managed, safeguarded, or secured in the context of certain activities or decisions, effective normative limits must intervene *before* data enters the equation.

In other words, our continued emphasis on regulating the privacy, security, and management of personal data, without any prior limits on datafication, is an unsustainable proposition in the face of ever-invasive new and advanced technologies that are transforming the relationship between humans and machines. Without articulating natural and normative limits on datafication, already powerful corporations will only further weaponize privacy and data protection, turning them into the handmaidens of surveillance and control. Beyond data, and even beyond control over hardware and software, we must examine and challenge the legitimacy of the underlying narratives, techniques, and processes that support private power, including through direct limits on privatization.

Limits on Private Power

As I explored in chapter 4, dominant technology companies, such as Apple, Meta (Facebook), and Google, have been gradually enclosing online or virtual spaces by bringing all manner of products and services into their walled gardens through vertical integration and control. But as we transition into a postdigital, cyberphysical world where AI and machine learning are widely deployed to operate and manage all manner of activities and services, unchecked private power risks going beyond enclosing *online* services to actually walling off or enclosing *physical* spaces by bringing them under corporate incentives and control. The integration of these privately owned and operated digital tools and technologies into formerly public spaces risks the rendition and datafication of all experiences within them, threatening the very the nature of *public* or common spaces.

As we have seen, even when these companies are not collecting data about specific individuals, they are extracting insights that achieve the same ends—ends that perpetuate and extend their power and control over more and more domains of life. As Crawford observes in *Atlas of AI*, "The new AI gold rush consists of enclosing different fields of human knowing, feeling, and action—every type of available data—all caught up in an expansionist logic of never-ending collection. It has become a pillaging of public space."[49] As a result, meaningful limits on datafication and the rendering of human experience also require limits on the acceptable realm of private ownership and control, including on the enclosure of the commons and public spaces, in order to protect individuals and communities.

The pillaging of the commons is another long-standing cause and effect of all forms of colonialism, including data colonialism. From a historical perspective, Couldry and Mejias explain how "data colonialism completes the process of appropriating life that the expropriation of nature started." They further posit that "the effect of data colonialism . . . is to give corporations control of resources that can be extracted from social life by installing into people's lives corporate powers and rights of surveillance that did not exist before. The result is to appropriate human life to corporate power and thus dispossess it of its independent agency."[50] These corporate powers and rights of surveillance are increasingly supported by the transfer and adaptation of what were traditionally conceived of as individual human rights to private corporations, such as the freedom of speech or expression.

In a 2010 landmark decision in a case regarding campaign finance laws, the US Supreme Court ruled that the First Amendment prevents the government from restricting how much companies and other entities can spend on political ads and campaigns.[51] Since then, corporations have been expanding the corporate free speech doctrine to protect all manner of invasive activities in connection with emerging technologies. Controversial facial recognition company Clearview AI, for example, has defended its scraping of three billion images from the internet to feed into its AI-enabled biometric tools sold to law enforcement agencies on the basis that the company has a First Amendment right to capture the facial prints of individuals without their consent and that such activity constitutes constitutionally protected speech.[52]

This increasing privatization or usurpation of rights by corporations is a threat to individuals, communities, and society at large.

The more these corporate powers and rights expand, the more the institutions we rely on for the realization and protection of our fundamental rights decay. As Rebecca MacKinnon argued more than a decade ago in her prescient book *Consent of the Networked*, governance for a globally interconnected digital world, in a way that constrains the abuse of both government and corporate power while protecting individual rights, must be rooted in the consent of the networked to be legitimate and effective.[53] But governance is increasingly undermined by the complexity and opacity of privately owned and operated technologies deployed in public settings or procured by public entities in the provision of government services.

As the private sector increases its influence through wealth accumulation along with growing control over critical infrastructure and other dependencies, governments gradually cede power and lose control over their sovereign functions. Effective governance must address the increasingly opaque and unaccountable relationships between governments and private companies that own and operate the digital networks and platforms on which our democracies depend, constrain that power, and hold it accountable. At some point, antimonopoly, antitrust, and competition measures, including specific interventions designed to address vertical integration through control over infrastructure, must also become part of the solution for curbing the power of these companies. Failing such a comprehensive approach, private power will not only pose a threat to people, as individuals and communities, but will increasingly threaten governments and the social contract too.[54] Continuing to overly rely on data-based interventions is a recipe for disaster.

Defining the Limits of Permissible Datafication

So far in this chapter, I have examined the natural and normative limits of datafication. Natural limits include instances where rendering experience into data is simply not yet, and perhaps never will be, technologically feasible, while normative limits have to do with resisting the commodification of everything by imposing moral limits on markets and privatization. Nevertheless, so long as digital technologies remain, we will still have to grapple with datafication, not because the datafication of *everything* is acceptable or inevitable, but because the datafication of *some things* is.

In some cases, datafication may even be desirable or beneficial. For instance, few would argue against the use of advancements in neurotechnologies to restore vision or aid with the rehabilitation of stroke victims, where provably effective. As such, we might agree that the datafication of cognitive or neurological processes and thoughts can be permissible, depending on the ultimate ends or purposes of that datafication. Despite their desirability, such uses still come with unprecedented levels of risk and the potential for significant abuse.

In these cases, where datafication may be permissible or even beneficial, we still need to impose limits by prenegotiating and articulating those permissible purposes, such as the use of neuro-technologies in support of medical research, when narrowly defined and in the public interest. We will also need to set ex ante rules and requirements around datafication for those limited purposes, impose liability and consequences for the harms that may result, and implement mitigation and remediation strategies. This is especially the case when carried out by for-profit entities. The hope is that limits on what is permissible, combined with other rules and requirements that go beyond the mere privacy and security of data, will provide more robust protections that better match the nature of threats to human dignity, privacy, identity, autonomy, and integrity in a postdigital, cyberphysical world.

But that still leaves us with a need to articulate and design a framework for setting those ex ante rules on permissible datafication, identifying the nature of the harms at play, and defining potential methods of remediation. Just as we do with building codes, health and safety regulations for food, drugs, and drinking water, and across other domains, we cannot place this burden on any single individual or even any group of individuals, and critically, we cannot start from the perspective of data. The next chapter explores how a human rights–based approach can help shift the burden off individuals, and onto the organizations and entities that control the underlying processes of, benefit most directly from, and create the majority of risks associated with datafication.

7

Back to the Future: A Return to Human Rights

In the brave new, postdigital, cyberphysical world that we are coming to inhabit, our overreliance on data protection and data-centric privacy frameworks as tools of effective technological governance is failing us. In turn, we are increasingly exposed and vulnerable in the face of ever-expanding private power, sustained in part by the exceptional treatment of "technology companies." In the previous chapter, I explored why effectively reining in this power requires us to go beyond data by intervening before *personal data* is implicated, and in some cases, even before *data* enters the equation. This approach involves identifying the natural limits of datafication and rendition, imposing normative limits on both, including through limits on markets and privatization, and defining the scope of and rules for permissible datafication. But even recognizing the need for these measures does not tell us *where* those limits should lie or *what* the rules should be.

For that, we must go back to the future. Specifically, we must return to the original human rights–based conceptualizations of privacy and data protection, before they took an ICT turn, to a framework focused on protecting *people* rather than merely ensuring the privacy or security of *data*. Although the application of human rights to digital technologies is not without precedent, the conversation to date has largely revolved around a narrow subset of individual rights, specifically privacy and free expression. This limited application of human rights is due in part to the dominance of Western values in the early design, development, and deployment of the internet and digital technologies as well as the ongoing dominance of US technology companies over digital infrastructure globally.

A narrow focus on privacy and expression may have made sense in the old view of the digital realm as one separate and apart from the "real world"—a realm neatly confined to the domain of ICT. But it makes little sense in the postdigital, cyberphysical world in which data, constituting the built environment and increasingly commingled with our physical being, cannot provide a stable anchor for technology governance. Rather, we must ground ourselves in something more fundamental—namely a human rights framework that centers people. In fact, human rights are arguably more relevant now than at any point since their inception as new technologies challenge what it means to be human, and yet they are often dismissed as irrelevant.

This chapter examines the limited application of human rights to digital technologies to date, the breadth of human rights implicated by emerging technologies in a postdigital world, and the need to recalibrate our application of human rights to renew their relevance in addressing the increasing complexity of challenges we face. It also explores how such a recalibration may require us to reevaluate and adapt existing rights as well as potentially introduce new ones. The hope is that a more robust human rights framework can provide a backstop against runaway extraction and commodification, while helping to rebuild international consensus around the norms that should govern our relationship to technologies in a brave new world.

Human Rights and Technology Governance

As I explored in part I, modern human rights law emerged nearly seventy-five years ago in the wake of World War II with the adoption of the UDHR in 1948. Today, there are more than thirty distinct human rights and freedoms recognized by international human rights law, and dozens more recognized in regional and other frameworks. And yet the conversation with regard to human rights and digital technologies has largely been reduced to a narrow set of two rights: privacy and the freedom of expression.[1] In fact, until recently, the conversation was actually dominated by a near singular focus on the latter. For example, Article 19 of the International Covenant on Civil and Political Rights (ICCPR), on the freedom of expression, plays a significant role in the public debate over content moderation on large digital platforms and even features in the name of a prominent international digital rights advocacy organization.[2] This narrow approach is partly the result of history and partly due to intentional strategies by dominant corporations to narrow the scope of the conversation about governance.

From a historical perspective, the UDHR incorporated a wide array of principles relating to *civil and political rights* (CPRs) as well as *economic, social, and cultural rights* (ESCRs), which at the time, were considered to be deeply interrelated and inextricably linked.[3] CPRs are often regarded as "negative" rights and freedoms that ensure an individual's right to participate in civil and political life without discrimination, repression, or interference by the state. They include the well-known individual rights to life, liberty, and privacy, the freedoms of thought, conscience, and religion, and the freedoms of expression, association, and assembly as well as general rights to nondiscrimination and equal protection. Such rights are commonly articulated in Western constitutional traditions, including the US Constitution's Bill of Rights. They also echo in the cyberlibertarian ethos captured by John Perry Barlow's "A Declaration of the Independence of Cyberspace," which declared the internet to be a place of negative freedoms, devoid of interference by the state.[4]

ESCRs, which are sometimes regarded as more "positive" and "collective" in nature, are concerned with the basic social and economic conditions necessary to enable individuals to live a life of dignity and freedom. They are rights related to employment, social security, family life, access to healthcare and education, adequate living standards (such as access to food, clothing, and housing), the environment, and participation in cultural life.[5] In some ways, ESCRs are foundational or primary, being necessary for the actual enjoyment of CPRs.[6] Nevertheless, they require progressive realization, which depends on the resources of a state as well as international assistance and cooperation.[7]

Despite sharing a common source in the UDHR, Cold War politics led to Western states prioritizing and emphasizing CPRs in the ensuing decades, while Eastern states largely championed ESCRs.[8] This division resulted in the execution of two separate, legally binding instruments in 1966: the ICCPR, and the International Covenant on Economic, Social and Cultural Rights (ICESCR). Together with the UDHR, they form what is known as the International Bill of Human Rights. Several subsequent international human rights law instruments, such as the Convention on the Rights of the Child and the Convention on the Rights of Persons with Disabilities, incorporate both CPRs and ESCRs without clear demarcation between them.[9] Nevertheless, early adopters of computers and other digital technologies, including the United States, United Kingdom, Norway, and other Western European nations, emphasized CPRs in contrast to the focus on ESCRs in Communist states.

While the distinction between negative and positive rights is an oversimplification, as so-called negative rights and freedoms may yet require the state to take active measures beyond just refraining from action, including to take affirmative steps to legally enforce such rights, it is conceptually useful in the context of early digital rights.[10] Similarly, the lines between CPRs and ESCRs are not as clean as separate instruments would suggest, with both featuring negative and positive dimensions, ensuring certain freedoms *from* the state and certain freedoms *through* the state. They are also not as neatly distinguishable as individual or collective rights, with both having individual and collective aspects. While it is increasingly recognized that human rights are critical to the conversation about digital technologies, particularly with respect to risks of exclusion and discrimination,[11] ESCRs remain vastly underappreciated, as do the more positive or affirmative aspects of rights and freedoms traditionally conceived of as negative, such as the right to privacy.

As the internet evolved from a technical research network into the foundations of a predominantly for-profit venture known as the commercial web, large technology firms were incentivized to narrow the scope of human rights as applied to the "online" or digital realm. The dominance of US companies over digital infrastructure would lead to a narrow emphasis on the freedom of expression and a largely First Amendment–inspired interpretation of expression at that.[12] When the zeitgeist shifted to an obsession with data, so too did these companies jump onboard to welcome a narrow interpretation of privacy focused primarily on the security and confidentiality of data. Today, both rights—free expression and privacy—are frequently emphasized as the pillars of "digital rights" in industry talking points as well as the benchmarks for human rights assessments of these firms by civil society and advocacy groups.[13]

When you start from the perspective of *data*, it is easy to see how a vast corpus of human rights law quickly gets whittled down to just a few individual rights. In turn, this automatically narrows the potential relevance and scope of protection afforded by a human rights framework with respect to new and advanced digital technologies, making such a framework easier to dismiss or devalue. On the other hand, when you begin from the perspective of *people*, metaversal technologies such as XR, emotion and affect recognition technologies, neurotechnologies, digital identity systems, and myriad other emerging technologies implicate a much broader array of human rights, including ones traditionally characterized as CPRs and ESCRs, as further explored below. It then becomes easier to see the potential value, potency, and enduring sustainability of a human rights–based approach to technology governance.

Human Rights and the Metaverse

Without question, new and advanced technologies such as emotion detection and affect recognition technologies, neurotechnologies, and XR and other metaversal technologies, among others, raise significant privacy-related concerns. In chapter 5, I outlined how each new category of technology penetrates a layer deeper into our personal space, threatening to erode the boundaries of our inner lives and inner selves. Moreover, the rendering and datafication of these activities into digital information raises traditional and novel data protection concerns, despite the inadequacies of existing laws that pertain to personal data and frequently require the identifiability of individuals. And whereas conventional legal frameworks typically regard privacy as an individualistic concern, new and emerging technologies increasingly have implications for individuals, groups, and society as a whole too.

XR technologies are a clear example of the simultaneously personal and collective nature of these privacy concerns. In order to fuse virtual and physical or "real-world" components together, XR technologies typically involve the collection and use of biometric identifiers and measurements, real-time location tracking, and "always-on" audio and video recording technologies that create detailed, live maps and models of spaces or places and record ambient sounds. From the perspective of an individual using the technology, XR devices tend to capture information about the individual's voice or vocal tone, iris, pupil movements and gaze, gait and other body movements, location information, device information and identifiers, and more, raising obvious concerns about the privacy and security of data harvested about that individual.[14] These practices also raise concerns about the personal privacy and security of individuals insofar as these technologies can be used to track and surveil them.

Apart from the privacy risks to an individual using these technologies, such as by wearing an XR headset or glasses, they introduce significant risks to nonusers and other people who may be implicated through interactions with that individual in both the virtual and physical worlds. For example, "always-on" recording devices and cameras are likely to capture the images, movements, voice, conversations and other sounds of unknowing and unwitting bystanders. Where combined with advanced biometric identification systems, such as facial or voice recognition technologies, they might also locate and specifically identify individuals in the surrounding area without their knowledge or consent, and in turn, without any opportunity to opt out. At present, there are few laws or regulations that account for these scenarios. As a result, as the Electronic Frontier Foundation cautions, we could end up in a "global panopticon society of constant surveillance in public or semi-public spaces."[15] XR technologies illustrate the contextual and interpersonal nature of our privacy challenges too, and the need for a more collective approach in a postdigital world.

But the concerns with respect to metaversal technologies such as XR run much deeper than what we traditionally conceive of as privacy challenges. These technologies are, by definition, designed to *alter* or *extend* reality. As such, they are inherently powerful tools for manipulation and discrimination. Depending on the reality individuals are exposed to, they might be persuaded, manipulated, or coerced into choices, behaviors, or activities against their own best interests, and often unknowingly. While this phenomenon already exists in the digital media and information landscape, such as with respect to algorithmic systems for personalization and behavioral targeting, XR and similar technologies could further amplify and exacerbate the so-called *filter bubble* effect.[16] Moreover, individuals who exist in the same physical space may experience different versions of "reality," depending on their gender, race, socioeconomic status, and other protected or sensitive attributes (and, potentially, depending on their ability to pay for the latest or best XR technologies). In these ways, such technologies pose a direct threat to the values of personal autonomy, human dignity, choice, consent, and self-determination—values that often underlie concerns about privacy and are central to functioning democratic societies.

Emotion Recognition, Neurotechnologies, and Human Rights

As anyone who has ever meditated can attest, thoughts and emotions arise spontaneously and unconsciously, and are frequently outside of our control. Should the automatic or passive observation or collection of thoughts and feelings through neurotechnologies that can "read" the brain, or emotion detection and affect recognition technologies that seek to infer mental or emotional states from physical or physiological properties, become possible, such activities would threaten our privacy, broadly construed. Should these technologies be deployed for general purposes in public settings, people would lack any control over, or opportunity to consent or object to, sensitive information collected or inferred about them, and there would be significant risks associated with the unauthorized use or disclosure of this information. This is, for example, why the use of general facial recognition technologies has been so fervently contested and opposed by people everywhere, leading a growing number of cities and municipalities to ban their use partially or even entirely.[17]

While emotion detection and recognition technologies and neu-rotechnologies both undoubtedly raise privacy and data protection–related concerns, their human rights implications run much deeper still. For instance, international and regional human rights laws recognize a right to the freedom of thought and conscience, and the freedom from coercion to have or adopt certain beliefs.[18] As a corollary to the frequently cited freedom of expression, international human rights law recognizes a freedom to hold opinions, expressed in the ICCPR as "everyone shall have the right to hold opinions without interference."[19] While these rights were articulated and codified long before the introduction of modern emotion recognition or neurotechnologies, and make no mention of the technological modes or means of interfering with these rights, they are no less relevant to them.

Without the intervention of digital technologies, our thoughts, feelings, and emotions are aspects of ourselves that arise and are initially unexpressed, if and until we decide to express them. The decision to express them outwardly (or not) is central to personal dignity and autonomy, or "the presumption that one is a person whose actions, thoughts and concerns are worthy of intrinsic respect, because they have been *chosen, organized* and *guided*."[20] But technologies that seek to harvest, render, and datafy our thoughts, feelings, and emotions, particularly by passive or automatic means, may coerce the expression of these unexpressed aspects of ourselves, in contravention of several human rights, including the freedom of thought and conscience, which includes freedom from coercion as well as the freedom to hold opinions without interference. Moreover, to the extent that these technologies are used or deployed to rank or score people, make consequential determinations about their rights to access or receive certain information or services, or restrict their ability to participate in certain activities on the basis of such spontaneous phenomena, they could coerce the adoption of particular beliefs or interfere with free association and assembly, among other rights.

Individual liberty and autonomy are also threatened by these technologies insofar as they expand the scope of experiences by which others might influence our decision-making, such as our emotions, moods, or thoughts. According to the NeuroRights Initiative at Columbia University, "Neurotechnology raises unique ethical concerns, because, unlike predecessor technologies, it directly interacts with and affects the brain."[21] Beyond increasing the complexity of the privacy and security challenges, human agency is threatened to the extent that these technologies can be used to interfere with or influence our decision-making or control our thoughts (sometimes referred to as *mind control*). Where personalized and targeted behavioral advertising poses serious risks to the right to privacy along with the freedoms of thought and expression, neurotechnologies amplify these risks by an order of magnitude, while introducing new risks with respect to manipulation, nonconsensual brain reading or *neurohacking*, and more.

Depending on their use or application, emotion recognition and neurotechnologies may also implicate the freedom against self-incrimination and right to due process, while threatening rights to nondiscrimination and equal protection. For example, the use of these technologies in judicial, legal, or law enforcement contexts, particularly where thoughts, feelings, or emotions are used to infer or ascribe criminal intent or guilt, raises serious human rights concerns.[22] What if my emotions, say, cause me to visualize harming someone, even if I have no intention of acting on these thoughts or feelings? What if someone manipulates me into committing a crime or implants false memories of having committed one? What if these technologies are utilized in precrime or predictive policing tools, especially with known concerns and limitations with respect to racial, gender, and other biases? While they might seem like science fiction scenarios (and for now, largely are), these types of questions are nevertheless essential to understanding and articulating the human rights–related risks and concerns of such technologies should they become capable, or perhaps more likely, when treated *as if* they were capable, of performing these activities. They raise deeper concerns regarding human dignity too.

As our bodies are increasingly scanned and surveilled by technologies in an attempt to infer internal states, we risk drawing unwanted and excessive attention to behavior and the body, increasing self-consciousness, social anxiety, and the objectification of self. As one scholar observes, emotion detection and affect recognition technologies present unique risks that "people may be treated as emotional animals to be biologically mapped and manipulated [or] seen as objects rather than as subjects."[23] These risks are present even absent direct intervention or manipulation. Just as research has shown that we behave differently when we are being watched, with significant implications for the social and behavioral influence of surveillance, we may also be influenced to think or feel differently should our thoughts or feelings become automatically or passively observed or inferred through the use of these technologies.[24] For some individuals or groups, such capabilities would threaten their ability to participate in the social or cultural life of their communities or societies should they have minority or dissenting views, opinions, or preferences. The commodification of our thoughts and feelings once rendered and datafied through emotion recognition and neurotechnologies subjects these spheres of experience to manipulation and exploitation for profit, and often against our own best interests, further threatening human dignity.

Digital Identity and Human Rights

Digital identity technologies are another class of technologies that implicates a broad array of human rights despite a narrow focus on the privacy and data protection concerns they have raised to date. At present, the public conversation about human rights with respect to a given digital identity tool or technology typically begins by evaluating its specific technical features or functionality, particularly the degree to which a given tool protects the privacy or security of data.[25] As discussed in chapter 4, this phenomenon was on heightened display during the COVID-19 pandemic in the public debates and discourses over whether digital identity-based tools, such as contact tracing or exposure notification apps, should feature a centralized or decentralized technical architecture, and later in the pandemic, over the privacy implications of digital proof-of-vaccination tools. This framing is an example of an approach that is both exceedingly narrow and simultaneously overreaching from a human rights perspective.

While privacy is a fundamental right recognized under international human rights law, it is not absolute. Rather, it is subject to certain derogations, including, most relevant in a pandemic, "for the protection of public health and morals," so long as such derogations are prescribed by law, necessary to achieve a legitimate aim, and proportionate to the aim pursued.[26] When assessing the potential human rights impacts of a given technological tool or solution, the starting point must be the context for introducing it. Before debating whether a contact tracing app should be centralized or decentralized, for instance, the human rights framework would have us ask whether such an app will be efficacious in preventing or slowing the spread of a disease, or supporting the public health response more generally. If there is no evidence for its efficacy in relation to these objectives, it would fail to satisfy the tests for necessity and proportionality, and any trade-offs with respect to privacy are false ones.

But new and emerging technologies also raise a host of human rights–related concerns that go beyond those addressed by data protection and privacy frameworks. Specifically, digital technologies increasingly pose serious risks of exclusion in ways that threaten both CPRs and ESCRs. For example, digital and phygital identity tools, including pandemic technologies such as digital proof-of-vaccination apps, implicate personal autonomy, the freedoms of association, assembly, and movement, and the right to work or attend school as well as the right to participate in social or cultural life. Based on underlying inequities, such as uneven access to vaccines or smartphones, they pose risks to the principles of equality and nondiscrimination too, and threaten the alienation of certain individuals or entire groups from public spaces or public life. When built on top of already discriminatory and exclusionary systems, the risks are further compounded.

Such risks are also amplified by digital and phygital identity technologies that incorporate the use of advanced physical and behavioral biometrics as well as opaque, inexplicable, and often proprietary AI tools and machine learning algorithms that exhibit bias or other dimensions of unfairness. Combined with newfound market dimensions and commercial incentives that distort the role of digital identity and increase its ubiquity, including by introducing identification requirements in contexts where previously not necessary or required, we may slowly erode the possibility of anonymity, including in "public" settings. The concerns here are collective, going beyond the identifiability of any single individual, to the general possibility of identifying people as increasingly machine-readable objects or data bodies. Where digital identity tools are further combined with other advanced technologies, such as emotion recognition or neurotechnologies, and/or delivered through new IoT and IoB devices, the human rights implications grow more heightened and complex.

Recalibrating Human Rights for a Postdigital World

As UN High Commissioner for Human Rights Michelle Bachelet observes, "The digital revolution is a major global human rights issue. Its unquestionable benefits do not cancel out its unmistakable risks."[27] New and advanced technologies clearly implicate a wide array of existing human rights as codified in the International Bill of Human Rights, going well beyond data protection and privacy or the freedom of expression. While many of those original rights remain relevant (and even more salient) today, they were designed to address threats then in existence, and do not entirely capture or contend with the nature of new threats we face to our experience of being human vis-à-vis technological developments in a postdigital, cyberphysical world. In other words, human rights *as presently articulated* are not entirely fit for purpose.

In order to demonstrate the relevance of human rights in a postdigital world, we need a recalibration of human rights at both the substantive and procedural level. As scholars William Schulz and Sushma Raman argue in *The Coming Good Society*, "If rights fail to be adapted to new realities, they will be eroded as readily by indifference and irrelevance as they are by defiance. . . . When established human rights are in jeopardy, it is more important than ever to ensure that rights are seen as responsive to contemporary problems.[28] Indeed, from a substantive perspective, we may need to reinterpret and adapt existing human rights, and potentially introduce new ones. In some cases, the line between reinterpreting existing rights and introducing new ones will be blurry as such "new" rights may be more akin to derivative ones, much like data protection is to the fundamental right to privacy.

One fundamental right that we urgently need to adapt is in fact the right to privacy, which has been emphasized as a core concern with respect to digital technologies and is sometimes even used as an umbrella term for as-yet articulated apprehensions about them.[29] In some respects, the introduction of a fundamental right to data protection, as in the European human rights tradition, was intended as an adaptation of the right to privacy, but as I have argued throughout this book, the hyperfocus on personal data makes data protection ill-equipped to address the full array of threats to human rights in the postdigital, cyberphysical world. As such, we may need to revisit privacy directly.

Under international human rights law, the right to privacy protects an individual from "arbitrary or unlawful" interferences with their "privacy, family, home, or correspondence."[30] While the physical domains or spheres of "family, home, and correspondence" are clear, and were widely included in national constitutions predating the UDHR and modern human rights law, the domain of *privacy* is not, and the reasons for including such a general right to privacy in these treaties is unclear.[31] To date, the application of the right to privacy to digital technologies has been rather limited and impeded by a near-singular focus on data (and specifically *personal information* or *personal data*). Nevertheless, the generality of the right should theoretically make it more durable and sustainable over time with some adaptation to new technological realities. As Schulz and Raman contend, "[The right to privacy] must be regularly revisited and updated in response to the changing realities around us."[32]

As already discussed, the postdigital, cyberphysical world, in which data comprises the built environment, makes it increasingly difficult and even impossible for any individual to opt out of the use or application of a specific technology, let alone the collection or processing of any personal data harvested through its application. As further explored in chapter 3, this reality has led numerous scholars to call for more collective *data* rights.[33] But the nature of generalized emotion detection and affect recognition technologies, behavioral and soft biometrics, and other advanced technologies, especially when deployed in public or common spaces, requires us to go beyond personal data and reinterpret the underlying right to privacy itself through a more collective lens.

Consider the use of emotion recognition technologies in public spaces such as smart cities. As Andrew McStay observes, "Given that over half the world's population lives in cities, many of which aim to become 'smart cities' . . . [c]onsideration should be given to *community privacy* to avoid a 'commodity logic' that both exceeds moral limits and corrupts the relationship between the individual and public life."[34] As with the growing machine readability of humans, rather than assessing the (data) privacy risks to any specific individual, we must confront questions about the kind of society we want to inhabit, and whether we value things like anonymity or obscurity, including whether we might need an actual right to anonymity in certain contexts.[35] Of course, the collective nature of these privacy concerns can also be interpreted as having to do with ESCRs, such as the right to participate in social or cultural life, particularly where certain individuals or groups may be more vulnerable or at risk without a degree of anonymity.[36]

Another fundamental right that would benefit from a recalibration or adaptation to demonstrate its relevance in a postdigital world is the freedom of thought and conscience, which has been much less prominent in the conversation about the governance of digital technologies than the right to privacy, even as it is potentially more protective. Whereas privacy is a qualified right subject to limitations or derogations under international human rights law, the freedom of thought is absolute, meaning that it cannot be interfered with under any circumstances.[37] But the absolute nature of this right is theoretical in the sense that the drafters of the International Bill of Human Rights could not have foreseen or imagined neurotechnologies or other modern technologies that actually threaten to penetrate the brain or purport to read internal states (whether they can, in reality, do so or not). In fact, the UDHR's drafters opined that "it would be unnecessary to proclaim freedom of [the inner sphere] if it were never to be given an outward expression" as the inner sphere is beyond reach.[38]

But the once unnecessary may become necessary in the face of new emotion detection and affect recognition technologies, neurotechnologies, and other technological innovations, or, perhaps more urgently, in the light of increasing belief in their capabilities. As I have already explored, technologies that attempt to render and datafy our internal mental and emotional states pose a clear threat to our freedom of thought and conscience as well as the freedom to hold opinions without interference or coercion, as they are inherently tools for manipulation and control. Just as our inner sphere may no longer be beyond reach in light of these new and advanced technologies, the absolute nature of the freedom of thought can no longer be taken for granted. As Schulz and Raman maintain, "As the world changes around us, new rights that may be hardly imagined today will come into being and some currently established rights will need to be reconceptualized."[39] Nevertheless, scholars disagree as to whether such technological developments necessitate new rights or merely require a reconceptualization of existing ones.

Researchers with the NeuroRights Initiative at Columbia University believe that "existing treaties cannot offer the robust and comprehensive human rights protection that a neurotechnological world requires." As such, they advocate for the creation of new human rights for the age of neurotechnology known as *neuro-rights*, which draw from underlying rights to privacy and freedom of thought. Alongside traditionally enumerated domains of privacy, such as family, home, and correspondence, for example, they argue that we may need to articulate something like a new "right to mental privacy, or the ability to keep thoughts protected against disclosure." They also call for additional neuro-rights to protect "the right to identity, or the ability to control both one's physical and mental integrity," and "the right to agency, or the freedom of thought and free will to choose one's own actions," which are more closely related to the fundamental right to freedom of thought and conscience.[40] Several countries, such as Chile and Spain, are beginning to undertake similar initiatives.[41]

Proposals for an array of new substantive rights related to the freedom of thought and conscience have also been characterized as rights to "mental self-determination," "cognitive liberty," and "psychological continuity."[42] Going beyond internal aspects of the freedom of thought, some scholars call for the freedom of thought to extend even to "external actions that are arguably constitutive of thought," such as reading, writing, or internet searches, as those protections are (at least as a matter of law) absolute and more protective than privacy protections.[43] But not everyone agrees that we need new rights. For example, legal scholar Susie Alegre argues that these proposed new rights actually "represent the practical development of the contours of freedom of thought in the 21st century," and that rather than introduce new rights, we simply need "clearer guidance and legal development of the meaning of the right to freedom of thought and opinion in the modern context and a more detailed legal framework to protect it."[44]

Such a legal framework might require procedural adjustments, like the creation of new infrastructure or the allocation of additional resources to support such legal development. Scholars with the NeuroRights Initiative, for example, advocate for procedural reforms, beginning with the formation of a new expert commission on neurorights within the United Nations, addition of special advisers with relevant expertise, and commencement of regular consultations with countries with advanced neurotechnology research programs.[45] In the longer term, they acknowledge the potential need for an entirely new international treaty focused on neuro-rights or at least a reinterpretation of existing treaties to address novel challenges, appointment of a special rapporteur on neuro-rights, and even the creation of a new human rights agency focused on the topic. Similar procedural recommendations might apply to the reconceptualization or adaptation of other fundamental rights beyond the right to privacy as well as the freedom of thought and conscience.

Finally, to better serve a globally connected world, future iterations of human rights in connection with digital technologies should seek to better balance more individualistic CPRs with more collective ESCRs, and rediscover their inherently interrelated nature, as originally envisaged by the UDHR, which did not differentiate between the two. New and advanced postdigital technologies, especially generalized technologies that are deployed in relation to groups of people or even the general public, pose mounting risks related to exclusion, discrimination, inequity, and insecurity, as do the algorithmic and automated processes used in decision-making about all aspects of our lives. As a result, ESCRs are conceptually more relevant now than at any time in history. And yet they have nearly disappeared from the digital rights conversation. As such, we may also need to reconceptualize ESCRs to demonstrate their importance.

For instance, as we are living in an age of constant connectivity and connection via digital tools and technologies, a growing labor movement is forming around a *right to disconnect*—essentially, a right of employees to disconnect from work by, say, not receiving or answering any work-related communications outside "normal" working hours—with national legislation underway in France, Spain, Luxembourg, and the Philippines, among other places.[46] Such a right would help protect and defend the boundedness of the individual, in the original spirit of the right to privacy under international human rights law. Importantly, though, it also draws on ESCR-style labor rights, including Article 24 of the UDHR, which provides that "everyone has the right to rest and leisure, including reasonable limitation of working hours," and Article 7 of the ICE-SCR, which recognizes "the right of everyone to the enjoyment of just and favourable conditions of work which ensure . . . [r]est, leisure and reasonable limitation of working hours."[47] One might also imagine such a right being leveraged to prevent numerous forms of surveillance of the personal sphere or domain via intrusive, data-hungry tools or technologies.

Of critical significance in a postdigital world, ESCRs emphasize equity and inclusion, and recognize the rights of everyone to "[enjoy] the highest attainable standard of physical or mental health," "take part in cultural life," and "enjoy the benefits of scientific progress and its applications," among others.[48] Adapting these rights to new and advanced technologies might require more specific articulation or enumeration in certain contexts. For example, with respect to neurotechnologies, the NeuroRights Initiative proposes the introduction of "the right to fair access to mental augmentation, or the ability to ensure that the benefits of improvements to sensory and mental capacity through neurotechnology are distributed justly in the population," and "the right to protection from algorithmic bias, or the ability to ensure that technologies do not insert prejudices."[49] While recalibrating human rights in this way is not without challenges, it still represents a more protective path than a continued focus on data-centric governance.

Human Rights as a Backstop against Commodification

Human rights are inherent and universal, attaching to all humans equally by virtue of their humanity alone. They are inalienable in the sense that they cannot be given or taken away, or bought or sold, nor do they depend on one's willingness or ability to pay. Human rights are not limited by commercial interests or economic incentives. Rather, they are primordial, coming before the market. Profit, for instance, does not factor into the necessity, proportionality, and legality tests. Moreover, there are no derogations for general commercial interests, or the promotion of trade or "innovation," despite the fact that these are oft-cited counterweights to the protection of individual rights under existing data protection and privacy frameworks.

States have a legal and moral duty to protect the full array of internationally recognized human rights contained in the International Bill of Human Rights, including CPRs enshrined in the

ICCPR and ESCRs set out in the ICESCR.[50] Separately and independently, businesses have a responsibility to respect them by avoiding causing or contributing to adverse human rights impacts linked to their activities, products, or services, and actively preventing or mitigating against them, as set out in the United Nations' Guiding Principles on Business and Human Rights.[51] Operationally, this requires businesses to publish and adopt a human rights policy, undertake human rights due diligence throughout their supply chains, and provide access to remedies, among other measures.[52]

As governments grow more dependent on the private sector for digital tools and technologies to aid with the provision of traditionally public services, including education, healthcare, and social services—a trend exacerbated and accelerated by the pandemic—commercial incentives are increasingly shaping our lived experiences in the postdigital world. While incumbent firms are growing increasingly cognizant of their independent responsibilities to *respect* human rights, large, globally dominant corporations that control a significant and increasing proportion of our digital infrastructure remain driven, first and foremost, by corporate commercial interests. Even the companies most renowned for respecting human rights are ultimately guided by their bottom line.[53] For example, they might provide heightened protections for individual rights such as privacy, but at a premium.[54]

Yet from a human rights perspective, this increasing reliance on the private sector does not provide an excuse to depreciate human rights. Rather, when relying on the private sector for the provision of goods and services essential for the exercise and enjoyment of fundamental rights, states ultimately remain responsible for ensuring noninfringement and protection of these rights.[55] States are also responsible for providing effective accountability and oversight of companies.[56] Given these features and characteristics of international human rights law, an expansive view of human rights in relation to digital technologies in a postdigital world provides an increasingly critical backstop against the commercialization of everything.

Moreover, as the idea of Web3 or the metaverse gains traction through blockchain-based applications, cryptocurrencies, and digital receipts known as *nonfungible tokens*—representing a shift from a content-based web supported by targeted ads to one in which every interaction becomes a financial transaction—this backstop only grows more critical. As author Ian Bogost observes, "First the internet made it easy for people to conduct their lives online. Then it made it possible to monetize the attention generated by that online life. Now the digital exhaust of all that life online is poised to become an asset class for speculative investment, like stocks and commodities and mortgages." Or more plainly, "the golden promise of Web3 is that every aspect of human life, as recorded by computers, will be collateralized."[57] For nearly three-quarters of a century, international human rights law instruments have spoken principle to power. And properly adapted to our modern technological reality, it is reasonable to believe that they can continue to do so for at least another three-quarters of a century, if not longer.

Human Rights and Consensus

While effective governance for cross-border technologies like the internet has always required a degree of international cooperation, the complexity of new and emerging (and increasingly borderless) technologies presents a heightened need for cross-border coordination and collaboration. As the European Data Protection Supervisor observed in relation to pandemic technologies such as mobile exposure notification apps, "Because the virus knows no borders, it seems preferable to develop a common European approach in response to the current crisis, or at least put in place an interoperable framework."[58] Similarly, the World Health Organization noted that "the ability to uniquely identify an individual and validate vaccination status requires international cooperation, orchestration across complex systems, and widespread adoption of open interoperability standards to support secure data access or exchange."[59]

Even before the pandemic, the digital realm was splintering, with rising data nationalism, and nation-states, authoritarian and democratic alike, turning toward digital or technological sovereignty, undermining efforts at coordination or cooperation.[60] However imperfect, international human rights law remains the closest thing we have to a broad international consensus for norms to govern society in general, including our evolving relationship to technology. For example, the ICCPR has been adopted by 173 countries, covering more than 90 percent of the world's population, while the UDHR has been adopted by the 193 countries of the United Nations and translated into 524 languages, making it the most widely translated document in the world. Another hard-fought consensus around the duty of corporations to respect human rights has already been articulated in the Guiding Principles on Business and Human Rights along with the corresponding duty of states to hold them accountable.

And yet human rights are in jeopardy around the world, largely because we have forgotten their relevance. As they predate digitalization and datafication, human rights can sometimes appear to be antiquated or incompatible with the modern technologically enhanced world, and are especially undervalued in the conversation about the governance of digital technologies and, soon, the post-digital reality. As explored in this chapter, we can restore their relevance through a recalibration focused on adapting existing rights, potentially introducing new (or more accurately, derivative) ones, and providing practical and institutional support. We must move beyond a limited application of human rights that emphasizes narrowly conceptualized rights to privacy and free expression over and above all others—an application historically shaped by globally dominant Western technology companies and viewed through an outdated ICT lens. And we must restore balance between CPRs and ESCRs by recognizing their inherent complementarity and interrelatedness. Without this kind of recalibration, we risk incentivizing more authoritarian approaches to digital technologies.

Just as the origins of modern data protection law for digital data emanated from the right to privacy under international human rights law, human rights are our best hope at establishing a new consensus for technology governance in a postdigital world, akin to the broad international consensus that formed around the FIPPs in the database age. Rooting the governance of new and advanced technologies in a human rights framework allows us to start from the perspective of *people* rather than from the vantage point of data, technology, commerce, or the market. As they are first and foremost about *humans*, human rights represent true human centricity, and not the diluted kind peddled by powerful authoritarian or commercial interests. Through this approach, we just might begin to break free of the data impasse we find ourselves in today, at the dawn of the metaverse (whatever shape it may ultimately take), and envision a future beyond data.

Acknowledgments

With the benefit of hindsight, I can trace the roots of this book back to my undergraduate days at Harvard and my former classmate Mark Zuckerberg. Since then, many more people than I can name here have shaped and inspired my thinking on data, human rights, and technology.

Nevertheless, I want to acknowledge my friends and colleagues at the Berkman Klein Center for Internet and Society (especially my Border Café crew), the Carr Center for Human Rights Policy at the Harvard Kennedy School (especially the ever-inspiring Sushma Raman), the Digital Civil Society Lab at Stanford (particularly the endlessly supportive Lucy Bernholz), and the Institute for Ethics in AI at Oxford University (especially John Tasioulas for encouraging my work on technology and human rights). For shaping these insights and inspiration into an actual book, I want to thank David Weinberger for early exploratory conversations and encouragement, Ben Green for sharing his perspective on what makes a successful book proposal, the anonymous reviewers who provided insightful feedback and suggestions on my manuscript, my production editor Deborah Cantor-Adams for making it read better, and my editor Gita Manaktala for taking a chance on a first-time author and for her guidance and support along the way.

In the time between the proposal and publication of this book, there were many personal and professional challenges, including the loss of loved ones and the challenging isolation of a global pandemic. I could not have made it through without the unwavering support of dear friends like Kata Kurilla, Doaa Mansour, Ian Mok, Erica Oppenheimer, Neal Cohen, Adam Yukelson, and Mimi Michailidi, and without my Delphi soul sisters who helped revive my spirit when I hit a seriously hard wall. With this book, as with everything else in my life, I would be nowhere without my parents, Eva and Jerry, and my brother, Chris, whose high expectations I am always looking to meet. I am also overcome with gratitude for my husband, Iain Fraser, for his constant encouragement, infinite patience, and ability to carry me through frequent waves of self-doubt.

Finally, this book, and all that I do, is for my departed grandparents, but especially mama and nagyapa, who taught me everything I know that really matters in life.

Notes

Prologue

1. See, e.g., collection of personal narratives, manuscripts, and ephemera about the 1918–1919 influenza pandemic (Collection 509), Louise M. Darling Biomedical Library History and Special Collections for the Sciences, University of California, Los Angeles.

2. European Commission, "Shaping Europe's Digital Future," February 19, 2020, https://ec.europa.eu/info/sites/default/files/communication-shaping-europes-digital -future-feb2020_en_4.pdf.

3. Regulation (EU) 2022/868 of the European Parliament and of the Council of 30 May 2022 on European data governance and amending Regulation (EU) 2018/1724 (Data Governance Act), PE/85/2021/REV/1, https://eur-lex.europa.eu/legal-content /EN/TXT/HTML/?uri=CELEX:32022R0868&from=EN.

4. Proposal for a Regulation of the European Parliament and of the Council on harmonised rules on fair access to and use of data (Data Act), COM/2022/68 final, https:// eur-lex.europa.eu/legal-content/EN/TXT/HTML/?uri=CELEX:52022PC0068&from=EN.

5. Regulation (EU) 2022/ . . . of the European Parliament and of the Council of [] on a Single Market For Digital Services (Digital Services Act) and amending Directive 2000/31/EC, PE-CONS No/YY - 2020/0361(COD), https://www.europarl.europa.eu /meetdocs/2014_2019/plmrep/COMMITTEES/IMCO/DV/2022/06-15/DSA_2020 _0361COD_EN.pdf (provisional text); Regulation (EU) 2022/ . . . of the European Parliament and of the Council on contestable and fair markets in the digital sector (Digital Markets Act), 2020/0374 (COD), https://www.consilium.europa.eu/media/56086 /st08722-xx22.pdf.

6. Proposal for a Regulation of the European Parliament and of the Council laying down harmonised rules on Artificial Intelligence (Artificial Intelligence Act) and Amending Certain Union Legislative Acts, COM/2021/206 final, https://eur-lex .europa.eu/legal-content/EN/TXT/HTML/?uri=CELEX:52021PC0206&from=EN.

7. Proposal for a Regulation of the European Parliament and of the Council laying down measures for a high common level of cybersecurity at the institutions, bodies, offices, and agencies of the Union, 2022/0085 (COD), https://ec.europa.eu/info/sites /default/files/proposal_for_a_regulation_laying_down_measures_on_cybersecurity _at_euibas.pdf.

8. American Data Privacy and Protection Act, H.R. 8152, 117th Congress, 2d session (June 21, 2022), https://www.congress.gov/bill/117th-congress/house-bill/8152/text.

9. Data Governance Act, recital 2 (emphasis added).

10. See Digital Governance Act, recital 7; Data Act, recital 8.

11. See Joseph Duball, "American Data Privacy and Protection Act Heads for US House Floor," IAPP, July 21, 2022, https://iapp.org/news/a/american-data-privacy -and-protection-act-heads-for-us-house-floor.

Introduction

1. Jeff Desjardins, "How Much Data Is Generated Each Day?," World Economic Forum, April 17, 2019, https://www.weforum.org/agenda/2019/04/how-much-data -is-generated-each-day-cf4bddf29f.

2. Verlyn Klinkenborg, "Opinion | Editorial Observer; Trying to Measure the Amount of Information That Humans Create," *New York Times*, November 12, 2003, https://www.nytimes.com/2003/11/12/opinion/editorial-observer-trying-measure -amount-information-that-humans-create.html.

3. See, for example, Stijn Prosper L. Christiaens, "The Internet of Things (IoT): Managing the Data Tsunami," *Collibra* (blog), accessed January 15, 2022, https://www .collibra.com/us/en/blog/the-internet-of-things-iot-managing-the-data-tsunami.

4. Brittany Kaiser, "Sign the Petition," Change.org, accessed January 15, 2022, https://www.change.org/p/tell-facebook-our-data-is-our-property-ownyourdata.

5. "The World's Most Valuable Resource Is No Longer Oil, but Data," *Economist*, May 6, 2017, https://www.economist.com/leaders/2017/05/06/the-worlds-most-valu able-resource-is-no-longer-oil-but-data; StJohn Deakins, "Data Is the New Water: Seven Reasons Why," *HuffPost UK*, October 12, 2017, https://www.huffingtonpost .co.uk/stjohn-deakins-/data-is-the-new-water-sev_b_18228184.html; Matt Loeb, "Data Is the New Air," CSO Online, May 23, 2018, https://www.csoonline.com/article /3275724/data-is-the-new-air.html; "Are Data More like Oil or Sunlight?," *Econo-*

mist, February 20, 2020, https://www.economist.com/special-report/2020/02/20/are
-data-more-like-oil-or-sunlight.

6. Eric A. Posner, E. Glen Weyl, and Vitalik Buterin, *Radical Markets: Uprooting
Capitalism and Democracy for a Just Society* (Princeton, NJ: Princeton University Press,
2019), chap 5; Julia Limitone, "Data Is the New Currency, Hewlett Packard Enter-
prise President Says," *FOX Business*, January 24, 2019, https://www.foxbusiness.com
/business-leaders/data-is-the-new-currency-hewlett-packard-enterprise-president-says;
Cory Doctorow, "Personal Data Is as Hot as Nuclear Waste," *Guardian*, January 15,
2008, https://www.theguardian.com/technology/2008/jan/15/data.security; Carissa
Véliz, *Privacy Is Power: Why and How You Should Take Back Control of Your Data*
(London: Melville House, 2021); Bruce Schneier, "Data Is a Toxic Asset—Schneier on
Security," March 4, 2016, https://www.schneier.com/blog/archives/2016/03/data
_is_a_toxic.html.

7. Shoshana Zuboff, *The Age of Surveillance Capitalism: The Fight for a Human Future
at the New Frontier of Power* (New York: Public Affairs, 2019), 65.

8. Kate Crawford, *Atlas of AI: Power, Politics, and the Planetary Costs of Artificial Intelligence* (New Haven, CT: Yale University Press, 2021).

9. Daniel Rosenberg, "Whence 'Data'?," *Berlin Journal*, no. 28 (Spring 2015): 18–22.

10. Rosenberg, "Whence 'Data'?"

11. Daniel Rosenberg, "Data before the Fact," in *"Raw Data" Is an Oxymoron*, ed.
Lisa Gitelman (Cambridge, MA: MIT Press, 2013), 20.

12. Rosenberg, "Whence 'Data'?," 21. ("Further scientific advance, Croker writes,
'must result, not from Fancy but from Facts, not from artfully devised Systems, but
from real Experiments'—from real experiments and facts, not from 'data.'")

13. See generally Lisa Gitelman, ed., *"Raw Data" Is an Oxymoron* (Cambridge, MA:
MIT Press, 2013).

14. Rosenberg, "Whence 'Data'?," 22.

15. Rosenberg, "Whence 'Data'?," 22.

16. Crawford, *Atlas of AI*, 113.

17. German Law Archive, "Federal Data Protection Act (Bundesdatenschutzgesetz,
BDSG)" (1977), § 2(I), https://germanlawarchive.iuscomp.org/?p=712.

18. See Regulation (EU) 2016/679 of the European Parliament and European Council of April 27, 2016, on the protection of natural persons with regard to the processing of personal data and the free movement of such data, and repealing Directive
95/46/EC (General Data Protection Regulation), OJ 2016 L 119/1, Art. 4(1) (hereafter
GDPR).

19. See California Consumer Privacy Act of 2018, Cal. Civ. Code § 1798.100 et seq. (2018) (hereafter CCPA).

20. See Data Protection Directive 95/46/EC of the European Parliament and European Council of October 24, 1995, on the protection of individuals with regard to the processing of personal data and the free movement of such data, OJ 1995 L 281/31 (hereafter the Directive).

21. GDPR, Art. 4(1). Cf. Directive, Art. 2(a), which defined *personal data* as "any information relating to an identified or identifiable natural person," and provided a short, nonexhaustive list of examples, including an "identification number" along with and information related to a person's "physical, physiological, mental, economic, cultural, or social identity."

22. See Regulation (EU) 2018/1807 on a framework for the free flow of non-personal data in the European Union, Reg. 2018/1807, Art. 3(1) (hereafter Non-personal Data Regulation), recitals ("'data' means data other than personal data as defined in point (1) of Article 4 of Regulation (EU) 2016/679").

23. Non-personal Data Regulation, recitals.

24. Directive, Art. 8(1).

25. GDPR, Art. 9(1). It also left significant wiggle room for member states to deviate from these categories according to their own national laws and preferences. See GDPR, recital 10. ("This Regulation also provides a margin of manoeuvre for Member States to specify its rules, including for the processing of special categories of personal data ['sensitive data']. To that extent, this Regulation does not exclude Member State law that sets out the circumstances for specific processing situations, including determining more precisely the conditions under which the processing of personal data is lawful.")

26. See, for example, CCPA, § 1798.140 (ae).

27. See, for example, Helen Fay Nissenbaum, *Privacy in Context: Technology, Policy, and the Integrity of Social Life* (Stanford, CA: Stanford Law Books, 2010). Nissenbaum rejects these dichotomies, dismissing any attempt to define a universally applicable definition of something like *sensitive information* as an impossible task, and instead advocates for a theory of privacy whereby the appropriate norms of all information flows are entirely contextual.

Chapter 1

1. Judith A. Swanson, *The Public and the Private in Aristotle's Political Philosophy* (Ithaca, NY: Cornell University Press, 1992).

2. See Griswold v. Connecticut, 381 U.S. 479 (1965).

3. See Elin Stensvand, "The Norwegian Constitution: From Autocracy to Democracy," University of Bergen, July 8, 2014, https://www.uib.no/en/news/79930/nor wegian-constitution-autocracy-democracy.

4. Hans Lien Braekstad, *The Constitution of the Kingdom of Norway, an Historical and Political Survey, with a Complete Translation of the Norwegian Constitution and the Act of Union between Norway and Sweden* (London: Wentworth Press, 2016).

5. See De Belgische Grondwet, Art. 10, Art. 22, https://www.senate.be/doc/const _nl.html.

6. Ursula Cristina Basset, ed., *Introduction to the Law of Argentina* (Alphen aan den Rijn, Netherlands: Wolters Kluwer, 2018), 97–98.

7. Finnish Constitution, 1919, Art. 11–12, https://finlex.fi/fi/laki/alkup/1919/1919 0094001. Translated with Google Translate.

8. See, for example, Judgment of June 16, 1969, 27 BVerfG I, 6; Judgment of May 6, 1973, 35 BVerfG 202, 221; Judgment of June 15, 1970, 27 BVerfG 344, 350.

9. Daniel Solove, "A Brief History of Information Privacy Law," in *Proskauer on Privacy: A Guide to Privacy and Data Security Law in the Information Age*, ed. Christopher Wolf (New York: PLI, 2006), 1–18.

10. Robert McMillan, "How Social Security Rescued IBM from Death by Depression," *Wired*, June 27, 2012, https://www.wired.com/2012/06/how-social-security -saved-ibm.

11. Wim Naudé and Paula Nagler, "Technological Innovation and Inclusive Growth," IZA Institute of Labor Economics, Discussion Paper Series No. 11194, December 2017, https://ftp.iza.org/dp11194.pdf.

12. Larry Frohman, "Population Registration, Social Planning, and the Discourse on Privacy Protection in West Germany," *Journal of Modern History* 87, no. 2 (June 1, 2015): 316–356, https://doi.org/10.1086/681304.

13. Frohman, "Population Registration."

14. See, for example, Jon Agar, *The Government Machine: A Revolutionary History of the Computer* (Cambridge, MA: MIT Press, 2003).

15. See, for example, Edwin Black, *IBM and the Holocaust: The Strategic Alliance between Nazi Germany and America's Most Powerful Corporation* (New York: Crown Publishers, 2001).

16. Agar, *Government Machine*, chap 6.

17. Linda Barnickel, "Spoils of War: The Fate of European Records during World War II," 1999, 7, https://minds.wisconsin.edu/handle/1793/45886.

18. Frans Viljoen, "International Human Rights Law: A Short History," United Nations, accessed January 15, 2022, https://www.un.org/en/chronicle/article /international-human-rights-law-short-history.

19. UN General Assembly, Universal Declaration of Human Rights, Resolution 217A, A/RES/3/217 A, December 10, 1948, Art. 12, https://www.un.org/en/about-us /universal-declaration-of-human-rights.

20. The reason for the explicit inclusion or reference to *privacy*, which was not found in national laws at the time, is unknown. Nevertheless, the inclusion of the term would influence subsequent national legislation and constitutions. See, for example, Oliver Diggelmann and Maria Nicole Cleis, "How the Right to Privacy Became a Human Right," *Human Rights Law Review* 14, no. 3 (September 1, 2014): 441–458, https://doi.org/10.1093/hrlr/ngu014.

21. International Covenant on Civil and Political Rights, December 19, 1966, 999 UNTS 171, Can TS 1976 No 47 (entered into force on March 23, 1976), Art. 17. ("1. No one shall be subjected to arbitrary or unlawful interference with his privacy, family, home or correspondence, nor to unlawful attacks on his honour and reputation. 2. Everyone has the right to the protection of the law against such interference or attacks.")

22. See UN Office of the High Commissioner for Human Rights, "The Right to Privacy in the Digital Age," June 30, 2014, https://digitallibrary.un.org/record/777869.

23. US Census Bureau, "UNIVAC I—History—U.S. Census Bureau," accessed January 15, 2022, https://www.census.gov/history/www/innovations/technology/univac _i.html.

24. Giovanni Dosi, "Institutions and Markets in High Technology: Government Support for Microelectronics in Europe," in *Industrial Policy and Innovation*, ed. Charles Frederick Carter (London: Heinemann Educational Books, 1981), 182–202.

25. See, for example, J. Lee Riccardi, "The German Federal Data Protection Act of 1977: Protecting the Right to Privacy?," *Boston College International and Comparative Law Review* 6, no. 1 (December 1, 1983): 243–271.

26. HEW Advisory Committee on Automated Personal Data Systems, *Records, Computers and the Rights of Citizens* (Washington, DC: US Department of Health, Education, and Welfare, July 1973).

27. See generally Solove, "A Brief History of Information Privacy Law."

28. Giovanni Navarria, "How the Internet Was Born: The ARPANET Comes to Life," *Conversation*, November 2, 2016, http://theconversation.com/how-the-internet-was -born-the-arpanet-comes-to-life-68062.

29. Katie Hafner and Matthew Lyon, *Where Wizards Stay up Late: The Origins of the Internet* (New York: Simon and Schuster Paperbacks, 2006).

30. Craig Timberg, "The Real Story of How the Internet Became So Vulnerable," *Washington Post*, May 30, 2015, http://www.washingtonpost.com/sf/business /2015/05/30/net-of-insecurity-part-1.

31. See, for example, J. Klensin, "Role of the Domain Name System (DNS)," *Informational Network Working Group* (blog), February 2003, https://datatracker.ietf.org/doc /html/rfc3467#section-1.1.

32. Hafner and Lyon, *Where Wizards Stay Up Late*, 248–249.

33. Graham W. Greenleaf, *Asian Data Privacy Laws: Trade and Human Rights Perspectives* (Oxford: Oxford University Press, 2014).

34. Gloria Gonzalez Fuster, *The Emergence of Personal Data Protection as a Fundamental Right of the EU* (Cham, Switzerland: Springer International Publishing, 2014), 56–57.

35. Gonzalez Fuster, *Emergence of Personal Data.*

36. Tore Dalenius, "Data Protection Legislation in Sweden: A Statistician's Perspective," *Journal of the Royal Statistical Society*, Series A (General) 142, no. 3 (1979): 285–298; Ian J. Lloyd, *Information Technology Law* (Oxford: Oxford University Press, 2020), 27.

37. Sören Öman, "Implementing Data Protection in Law," *Stockholm Institute for Scandinavian Law* 47, no. 18 (2004): 390–403.

38. Dalenius, "Data Protection Legislation in Sweden."

39. Riccardi, "The German Federal Data Protection Act of 1977," 248–267.

40. Act N°78–17 of January 6, 1978, on Information Technology, Data Files, and Civil Liberties, Commission nationale de l'informatique et des libertés, accessed April 15, 2022, https://www.cnil.fr/sites/default/files/typo/document/Act78-17VA .pdf [available in English at https://www.ssi.ens.fr/textes/a78-17-text.html].

41. Patrick Murray, "The Adequacy Standard under Directive 95/46/EC: Does U.S. Data Protection Meet This Standard?," *Fordham International Law Journal* 21, no. 3 (January 1, 1997): 932–1018.

42. Sarah L. Lode, "'You Have the Data' . . . The Writ of Habeas Data and Other Data Protection Rights: Is the United States Falling Behind?," *Indiana Law Journal* 94, no. 5 (2018): 41–63.

43. US Department of Health, Education, and Welfare, *Records, Computers, and the Rights of Citizens*, report of the HEW Advisory Committee on Automated Personal Data Systems, DHEW Publication No. (OS) 73–94, July 1973, https://www.justice .gov/opcl/docs/rec-com-rights.pdf (hereafter HEW Report).

44. HEW Report.

45. US Department of Justice, "Overview of the Privacy Act of 1974," February 24, 2021, https://www.justice.gov/archives/opcl/introduction.

46. 5 U.S.C. § 552a(b). In practice, the Privacy Act has been challenging to interpret and apply, and was largely a failure to operationalize until the Homeland Security Act of 2002. See, for example, Robert Gellman, "Fair Information Practices: A Basic History—Version 2.22," April 6, 2022, https://doi.org/10.2139/SSRN.2415020.

47. "Thirty Years After: The Impact of the OECD Privacy Guidelines," Organisation for Economic Co-operation and Development, March 10, 2010, https://www.oecd.org/sti/ieconomy/30yearsaftertheimpactoftheoecdprivacyguidelines.htm.

48. Convention for the Protection of Individuals with Regard to Automatic Processing of Personal Data, opened for signature January 28, 1981, ETS No. 108.

49. See, for example, W. Gregory Voss, "Obstacles to Transatlantic Harmonization of Data Privacy Law in Context," *Journal of Technology Law and Policy* 2 (2019): 405–463.

50. Asia-Pacific Economic Cooperation, *APEC Privacy Framework (2015)*, August 2017, https://www.apec.org/publications/2017/08/apec-privacy-framework-(2015).

51. Federal Trade Commission, *Privacy Online: A Report to Congress*, June 1998, https://www.ftc.gov/sites/default/files/documents/reports/privacy-online-report-congress/priv-23a.pdf.

Chapter 2

1. W. Gregory Voss, "Obstacles to Transatlantic Harmonization of Data Privacy Law in Context," *Journal of Technology Law and Policy* 2 (2019): 417.

2. See, for example, Justin Zobel, "The Computer Revolution: How It's Changed Our World over 60 Years," World Economic Forum, June 3, 2016, https://www.weforum.org/agenda/2016/06/the-computer-revolution-how-its-changed-our-world-over-60-years.

3. "U.S. Households with a Computer in the United States," Statista, February 1, 2010, https://www.statista.com/statistics/184685/percentage-of-households-with-computer-in-the-united-states-since-1984.

4. "UK Households: Ownership of Home Computers 1985–2018," Statista, December 7, 2020, https://www.statista.com/statistics/289191/household-penetration-of-home-computers-in-the-uk.

5. Andy Sloane and Felix van Rijn, *Home Informatics and Telematics: Information, Technology and Society* (New York: Springer, 2013), 102.

6. National Research Council, *Funding a Revolution: Government Support for Computing Research* (Washington, DC: National Academies Press, 1999).

7. "Internet History of the 1980s," Computer History Museum, accessed January 4, 2022, https://www.computerhistory.org/internethistory/1980s.

8. "From ARPANET to World Wide Web: An Internet History Timeline," Jefferson Online, November 22, 2016, https://online.jefferson.edu/business/internet-history -timeline.

9. "A Short History of the Internet," Science and Media Museum, December 3, 2020, https://www.scienceandmediamuseum.org.uk/objects-and-stories/short-history -internet#early-home-computers.

10. "A Short History of the Internet."

11. Don Tapscott, *The Digital Economy: Promise and Peril in the Age of Networked Intelligence* (New York: McGraw-Hill, 1996).

12. Treaty on European Union, February 7, 1992, 1992 O.J. (C191) 1, 31 I.L.M. 253.

13. See COM (90) 314 final—SYN 287 and 288, September 13, 1990, 4, https:// www.statewatch.org/media/documents/news/2014/sep/eu-2014-09-edps-data-pro tection-article.pdf. ("The diversity of national approaches and the lack of a system of protection at Community level are an obstacle to completion of the internal market. If the fundamental rights of data subjects, in particular their right to privacy, are not safeguarded at Community level, the cross-border flow of data might be impeded.")

14. Data Protection Directive 95/46/EC of the European Parliament and European Council of October 24, 1995, on the protection of individuals with regard to the processing of personal data and the free movement of such data, OJ 1995 L 281/31, recital 7 (hereafter the Directive).

15. Neil Robinson, Hans Graux, Maarten Botterman, and Lorenzo Valeri, *Review of the European Data Protection Directive* (Santa Monica, CA: RAND Corporation, 2009), https://ico.org.uk/media/1042349/review-of-eu-dp-directive.pdf.

16. Directive, recital 11 (acknowledging that the Directive was meant to "give substance to and amplify those contained in" Convention 108).

17. Directive, Art. 25(1), Art. 26.

18. US Federal Trade Commission, "Federal Trade Commission Enforcement of the U.S.-E.U. and U.S.-Swiss Safe Harbor Frameworks," December 2012, https://www.ftc .gov/tips-advice/business-center/guidance/federal-trade-commission-enforcement -us-eu-us-swiss-safe-harbor.

19. David Brett, "The Longest Bull Market in History: Five Charts That Tell the Story," Schroders, August 22, 2018, https://www.schroders.com/en/insights/eco nomics/the-longest-bull-market-in-history-in-five-charts.

20. Eugene N. White, "Bubbles and Bursts: The 1990s in the Mirror of the 1920s," National Bureau of Economic Research, Working Paper 12138, March 2006, https:// www.nber.org/system/files/working_papers/w12138/w12138.pdf.

21. White House, "Memorandum for the Heads of Executive Department Agencies, Subject: Electronic Commerce," July 1, 1997, https://fas.org/irp/offdocs/pdd-nec-ec .htm.

22. Fred H. Cate, "The Failure of Fair Information Practice Principles," in *Consumer Protection in the Age of the "Information Economy,"* ed. Jane K. Winn (Abingdon, UK: Routledge, 2006), 343.

23. In fact, these laws actually overemphasize *notice* over and above any notions of choice or consent. For example, the Health Insurance Portability and Accountability Act's Privacy Rule gives individuals a right to be informed of the privacy practices of their health plans and healthcare providers as well as their privacy rights with respect to their personal health information by requiring the entities covered by this act to provide a notice of privacy practices. See 45 C.F.R. 164.520.

24. Cate, "The Failure of Fair Information Practice Principles," 369.

25. John Perry Barlow, "A Declaration of the Independence of Cyberspace," Electronic Frontier Foundation, February 8, 1996, https://www.eff.org/cyberspace -independence.

26. Communications Decency Act, 47 U.S.C. § 230.

27. Barlow, "A Declaration."

28. For example, in recent congressional testimony, Mark Zuckerberg famously tes- tified that Facebook takes action to remove content on its platform when it could lead to imminent *real-world harm*, implying that activity on Facebook's platforms and properties occurs somewhere other than the real world. Mark Zuckerberg, "Hearing before the United States House of Representatives Committee on Energy and Commerce Subcommittees on Consumer Protection and Commerce and Com- munications and Technology," March 25, 2021, https://energycommerce.house .gov/sites/democrats.energycommerce.house.gov/files/documents/Witness%20 Testimony_Zuckerberg_CAT_CPC_2021.03.25.pdf.

29. April Glaser, "Another World Is Possible," *Logic Magazine*, August 3, 2019, https://logicmag.io/bodies/another-network-is-possible.

30. See generally Shoshana Zuboff, *The Age of Surveillance Capitalism: The Fight for a Human Future at the New Frontier of Power* (New York: Public Affairs, 2019).

31. Zuboff, *The Age of Surveillance Capitalism*, 211.

32. Voss, "Obstacles to Transatlantic Harmonization," 433.

33. European Commission, "Communication from the Commission to the European Parliament, the Council, the European Economic and Social Committee and the Committee of the Regions: A Digital Single Market Strategy for Europe," COM/2015/0192 final, May 6, 2015, https://eur-lex.europa.eu/legal-content/EN/TXT/?uri=celex%3A52015DC0192 (hereafter DSMS).

34. European Commission, "Commission Proposes a Comprehensive Reform of Data Protection Rules to Increase Users' Control of Their Data and to Cut Costs for Businesses," press release IP/12/46, January 25, 2012, https://ec.europa.eu/commission/presscorner/detail/en/IP_12_46.

35. DSMS, 145.

36. See, for example, Nitasha Tiku, "Europe's New Privacy Law Will Change the Web, and More," *Wired*, March 19, 2018, https://www.wired.com/story/europes-new-privacy-law-will-change-the-web-and-more.

37. Voss, "Obstacles to Transatlantic Harmonization."

38. Regulation (EU) 2016/679 of the European Parliament and European Council of April 27, 2016, on the protection of natural persons with regard to the processing of personal data and the free movement of such data, and repealing Directive 95/46/EC (General Data Protection Regulation), OJ 2016 L 119/1, Art. 1 (hereafter GDPR).

39. See, for example, Meg Leta Jones and Margot E. Kaminski, "An American's Guide to the GDPR," *Denver Law Review* 98, no. 1 (2021): 106–112; Gabriela Zanfir-Fortuna, "10 Reasons Why the GDPR Is the Opposite of a 'Notice and Consent' Type of Law," *Future of Privacy Forum*, September 13, 2019, https://fpf.org/blog/10-reasons-why-the-gdpr-is-the-opposite-of-a-notice-and-consent-type-of-law.

40. GDPR, Art. 4(11), Art. 7.

41. "Number of Sent and Received E-Mails per Day Worldwide from 2017 to 2025 (in Billions)," Statista, https://www.statista.com/statistics/456500/daily-number-of-e-mails-worldwide.

42. See, for example, "The Growth in Connected IoT Devices is Expected to Generate 79.4ZB of Data in 2025, According to new IDC Forecast," *Business Wire*, June 18, 2019, https://www.businesswire.com/news/home/20190618005012/en/The-Growth-in-Connected-IoT-Devices-is-Expected-to-Generate-79.4ZB-of-Data-in-2025-According-to-a-New-IDC-Forecast.

43. Laura DeNardis, *The Internet in Everything: Freedom and Security in a World with No Off Switch* (New Haven, CT: Yale University Press, 2020).

44. GDPR, recital 15. ("In order to prevent creating a serious risk of circumvention, the protection of natural persons should be *technologically neutral* and should not depend on the techniques used. The protection of natural persons should apply to the processing of personal data by automated means, as well as to manual processing, if the personal data are contained or are intended to be contained in a filing system" [emphasis added].)

45. See, for example, Douglas Busvine, Julia Fioertti, and Mathieu Rosemain, "European Regulators: We're Not Ready for New Privacy Law," Reuters, May 8, 2018, https://www.reuters.com/article/us-europe-privacy-analysis/european-regulators -were-not-ready-for-new-privacy-law-idUSKBN1I915X.

46. Ece Özlem Atikcan and Adam William Chalmers, "Choosing Lobbying Sides: The General Data Protection Regulation of the European Union," *Journal of Public Policy* 39, no. 4 (2019): 543–564.

47. US Department of Commerce, "Informal Comment on the Draft General Data Protection Regulation and Draft Directive on Data Protection in Law Enforcement Investigations," January 16, 2012, https://www.edri.org/files/US_lobbying 16012012_0000.pdf.

48. Lukas Schildberger, "Lobbying and Its Influence on the Draft of a General Data Protection Regulation of the European Union Unveiled in 2012" (master's thesis, Vienna University of Technology, May 30, 2016), https://www.law.tuwien.ac.at /Schildberger_Einreichversion.pdf.

49. Natasha Lomas, "Google among Top Lobbyist of Senior EC Officials," *TechCrunch*, June 24, 2015, https://techcrunch.com/2015/06/24/google-among-top-lobby ists-of-senior-ec-officials.

50. Schildberger, "Lobbying," 112.

51. Francesco Guarascio, "US Lobbying Waters Down EU Data Protection Reform," EURACTIV, February 21, 2012, https://www.euractiv.com/section/digital/news/us -lobbying-waters-down-eu-data-protection-reform.

52. GDPR, Art. 3.

53. Anu Bradford, *The Brussels Effect* (Oxford: Oxford University Press, 2020); Anu Bradford, "The Brussels Effect," *Financial Times*, January 27, 2020, https://www.ft .com/content/82219772-3eaa-11ea-b232-000f4477fbca.

54. "Mobile Operating Systems' Market Share Worldwide from January 2021 to June 2021," Statista, https://www.statista.com/statistics/272698/global-market-share -held-by-mobile-operating-systems-since-2009.

55. Felix Richter, "Amazon Leads $130 Billion Cloud Market," Statista, February 4, 2021, https://www.statista.com/chart/18819.

56. H. Tanovska, "Most Popular Social Networks Worldwide as of January 2021, Ranked by Number of Active Users," Statista, February 9, 2021, https://www.statista .com/statistics/272014/global-social-networks-ranked-by-number-of-users.

57. "Browser Market Share Worldwide: May 2020–May 2021," Statcounter, https:// gs.statcounter.com/browser-market-share.

58. See, for example, Nicole Perrin, "Facebook-Google Duopoly Won't Crack This Year," *eMarketer*, November 4, 2019, https://www.emarketer.com/content/face book-google-duopoly-won-t-crack-this-year.

59. Zuboff, *The Age of Surveillance Capitalism*, 352.

60. Ari Ezra Waldman, "Outsourcing Privacy," *Notre Dame Law Review* 96, no. 4 (2021): 195, 207.

61. See European Commission, *Joint Communication to the European Parliament and the Council: Towards a Comprehensive Strategy with Africa*, JOIN (2020) 4 final, March 9, 2020, https://ec.europa.eu/international-partnerships/system/files/communica tion-eu-africa-strategy-join-2020-4-final_en.pdf.

62. An example is the European Commission's recent adequacy decision with respect to Japan. See Elaine Fahey and Isabella Mancini, "The EU as an Intentional or Accidental Convergence Actor? Learning from the EU-Japan Data Adequacy Negotiations," *International Trade Law and Regulation* 2 (May 2020), https://ssrn .com/abstract=3606087. ("We contend that it is of significance and an important coincidence that *the adequacy decision was a side-product of the EU-Japan Economic Partnership Agreement* (EPA): despite the EU's initial goal of excluding data from the trade negotiations, Japan insisted on data dialogues and the EU eventually accom- modated the demands, hence triggering a process for an assessment of equiva- lence. . . . The EU-Japan efforts at reaching convergence provide a unique setting to study the EU as an emerging global legal actor in data" [emphasis added].)

63. See, for example, Christopher Mele, "Data Breaches Keep Happening. So Why Don't You Do Something?," *New York Times*, August 1, 2018, https://www.nytimes .com/2018/08/01/technology/data-breaches.html.

Chapter 3

1. See, for example, Cecilia Kang and Sheera Frenkel, "Facebook Says Cambridge Analytica Harvested Data of Up to 87 Million Users," *New York Times*, April 4, 2018, https://www.nytimes.com/2018/04/04/technology/mark-zuckerberg-testify -congress.html.

2. See, for example, Emma Graham-Harrison and Carole Cadwalladr, "Cambridge Analytica Execs Boast of Role in Getting Donald Trump Elected," *Guardian*, March

21, 2018, https://www.theguardian.com/uk-news/2018/mar/20/cambridge-analytica -execs-boast-of-role-in-getting-trump-elected.

3. See, for example, Julia Carrie Wong, "The Cambridge Analytica Scandal Changed the World—but It Didn't Change Facebook," *Guardian*, March 18, 2019, https:// www.theguardian.com/technology/2019/mar/17/the-cambridge-analytica-scandal -changed-the-world-but-it-didnt-change-facebook.

4. See, for example, Court Stroud, "Cambridge Analytica: The Turning Point in the Crisis about Big Data," *Forbes*, April 30, 2018, https://www.forbes.com/sites/court stroud/2018/04/30/cambridge-analytica-the-turning-point-in-the-crisis-about-big -data/?sh=6327516648ec.

5. "Americans and Privacy: Concerned, Confused and Feeling Lack of Control over Their Personal Information," Pew Research Center, November 15, 2019, https:// www.pewresearch.org/internet/2019/11/15/americans-and-privacy-concerned -confused-and-feeling-lack-of-control-over-their-personal-information.

6. "Personal Data," Google Trends, https://trends.google.com/trends/explore?date =today%205-y&q=%22personal%20data%22; "GDPR," Google Trends, https://trends .google.com/trends/explore?date=today%205-y&q=%22GDPR%22.

7. MyData.org.

8. California Consumer Privacy Act of 2018, Cal. Civ. Code § 1798.100 et seq. (2018).

9. Assembly Bill No. 713, California Consumer Privacy Act, Sec. 2(g), accessed April 18, 2022, https://leginfo.legislature.ca.gov/faces/billTextClient.xhtml?bill_id =201920200AB713.

10. See, for example, KJ Dearie, "Comparing the CCPA and the GDPR," *CPO Magazine*, March 26, 2020, https://www.cpomagazine.com/data-protection/com paring-the-ccpa-and-the-gdpr.

11. California Privacy Rights and Enforcement Act of 2020, amendments to version 3, November 4, 2019, https://oag.ca.gov/system/files/initiatives/pdfs/19-0021A1%20 %28Consumer%20Privacy%20-%20Version%203%29_1.pdf.

12. Neb. Rev. Stat. § 603A.300, accessed April 18, 2022, https://www.leg.state.nv .us/NRS/NRS-603A.html#NRS603ASec300; Virginia Consumer Data Protection Act, HB 2307, accessed April 18, 2022, https://lis.virginia.gov/cgi-bin/legp604.exe ?212+sum+HB2307; Senate Bill 21-190, A Bill for an Act concerning Additional Privacy Protection of Data Relating to Personal Privacy, First Regular Session, Seventy-Third General Assembly, State of Colorado, June 7, 2021, https://leg.colorado.gov /sites/default/files/documents/2021A/bills/2021a_190_rer.pdf.

13. National Conference of State Legislatures, "2019 Consumer Data Privacy Leg-islation," January 3, 2020, https://www.ncsl.org/research/telecommunications-and -information-technology/consumer-data-privacy.aspx.

14. National Conference of State Legislatures, "2020 Consumer Data Privacy Leg-islation," January 17, 2021, https://www.ncsl.org/research/telecommunications-and -information-technology/2020-consumer-data-privacy-legislation637290470.aspx.

15. National Conference of State Legislatures, "2020 Consumer Data Privacy Leg-islation," January 17, 2021, https://www.ncsl.org/research/telecommunications-and -information-technology/2020-consumer-data-privacy-legislation637290470.aspx; National Conference of State Legislatures, "2021 Consumer Data Privacy Legisla-tion," accessed April 18, 2022, https://www.ncsl.org/research/telecommunications -and-information-technology/2021-consumer-data-privacy-legislation.aspx.

16. Sarah Rippy, "US State Privacy Legislation Tracker," International Asso-ciation of Privacy Professionals, May 10, 2021, https://iapp.org/resources/article/us -state-privacy-legislation-tracker.

17. For example, a search for the terms *data governance, data management, data act, data privacy,* and *data protection* on GovTrack.us for the 116th Congress returns more than a hundred relevant results.

18. Adam Schwartz, "Two Federal COVID-19 Privacy Bills: A Good Start and a Misstep," Electronic Frontier Foundation, May 28, 2020, https://www.eff.org/deep links/2020/05/two-federal-covid-19-privacy-bills-good-start-and-misstep; Margaret Harding McGill, "Federal Privacy Legislation Shows Signs of Life in the House," *Axios,* December 19, 2019, https://www.axios.com/federal-privacy-legislation-shows -signs-of-life-in-house-e519ac0b-b512-47e1-8c84-aaf57d4144cf.html (with full text of the draft). Some of the most prominent proposals included the Consumer Data Privacy Act introduced by Senator Ron Wyden (D-OR), Data Care Act led by Senator Brian Schatz (D-HI), Data Accountability and Transparency Act put forth by Senator Sherrod Brown (D-OH), Consumer Online Privacy Rights Act proposed by Senator Maria Cantwell (D-WA), and Senator Kirsten Gillibrand's (D-NY) Data Protection Act in the Senate. Key proposals in the House included the Information Transpar-ency and Personal Data Control Act introduced by Representative Suzan DelBene (D-WA), and Online Privacy Act of 2019 proposed by Representatives Anna Eshoo (D-CA) and Zoe Lofgren (D-CA). See Consumer Online Privacy Rights Act, S. 2968, 116th Cong., 1st Sess. (December 3, 2019), https://www.congress.gov/116/bills /s2968/BILLS-116s2968is.pdf; Online Privacy Act of 2019, H.R. 4978, 116th Cong., 1st Sess. (November 5, 2019), https://www.congress.gov/116/bills/hr4978/BILLS -116hr4978ih.pdf.

19. For example, DelBene's law would have mandated that companies obtain *opt-in* consent before collecting data from consumers. See Information Transparency and

Personal Data Control Act, H.R. 2013, 116th Cong. (April 1, 2019), https://www
.congress.gov/bill/116th-congress/house-bill/2013/text.

20. See, for example, Michael Kwet, "In Stores, Secret Surveillance Tracks Your
Every Move," *New York Times*, June 14, 2019, https://www.nytimes.com/interac
tive/2019/06/14/opinion/bluetooth-wireless-tracking-privacy.html; Alfred Ng, "Contact Tracers concerned Police Tracking Protestors Will Hurt COVID-19 Aid," *CNET*,
June 1, 2020, https://www.cnet.com/news/contact-tracers-concerned-police-track
ing-protesters-will-hurt-covid-19-aid.

21. See, for example, Craig Timbert, "Brokers Use 'Billions' of Data Points to Profile Americans," *Washington Post*, May 27, 2014, https://www.washingtonpost.com
/business/technology/brokers-use-billions-of-data-points-to-profile-americans/2014
/05/27/b4207b96-e5b2-11e3-a86b-362fd5443d19_story.html.

22. Data Care Act, S. 2961, 116th Congress § 1 (2019), https://www.congress.gov/bill
/116th-congress/senate-bill/2961/text; Data Accountability and Transparency Act
of 2020 (Discussion Draft), 116th Congress, § 2 (2020), https://www.banking.senate
.gov/imo/media/doc/Brown%20-%20DATA%202020%20Discussion%20Draft.pdf.

23. Todd Feathers, "Big Tech Is Pushing States to Pass Privacy Laws, and Yes, You
Should Be Suspicious," *Markup*, April 15, 2021, https://themarkup.org/privacy
/2021/04/15/big-tech-is-pushing-states-to-pass-privacy-laws-and-yes-you-should-be
-suspicious.

24. Jill Cowan, "How Much Is Your Data Worth?," *New York Times*, March 25, 2019,
https://www.nytimes.com/2019/03/25/us/newsom-hertzberg-data-dividend.html.

25. Newmeyer Dillion, "Data Dividend? California Governor Proposes Plan to Have
Companies Pay Consumers for Using Their Info," *Lexology*, March 28, 2019, https://
www.lexology.com/library/detail.aspx?g=66214f93-276b-4d21-8ecc-b3a60ef24041.

26. "Data as a Property Right," Yang2020, accessed April 18, 2022, https://2020
.yang2020.com/policies/data-property-right (emphasis added).

27. See "What Is CDR?," Australian Government, accessed April 18, 2022, https://
www.cdr.gov.au/what-is-cdr.

28. James Meese, Punit Jagasia, and James Arvanitakis, "Citizen or Consumer? Con-
trasting Australia and Europe's Data Protection Policies," *Internet Policy Review* 8, no.
2 (2019), https://policyreview.info/articles/analysis/citizen-or-consumer-contrasting
-australia-and-europes-data-protection-policies.

29. European Commission, "A European Strategy for Data," Communication from
the Commission to the European Parliament, the Council, the European Economic
and Social Committee and the Committee of Regions, February 19, 2020, COM
(2020) 66 final, https://eur-lex.europa.eu/legal-content/EN/TXT/?qid=15930736856

20&uri=CELEX%3A52020DC0066; Proposal for a Regulation of the European Parliament and of the Council on European Data Governance (Data Governance Act), November 25, 2020, COM/2020/767 final, https://eur-lex.europa.eu/legal-content /EN/TXT/?uri=CELEX%3A52020PC0767 (hereafter DGA).

30. See DGA, recital 22.

31. Proposal for a Regulation of the European Parliament and of the Council on Harmonised Rules on Fair Access to and Use of Data (Data Act), February 23, 2022, COM/2022/68 final, https://digital-strategy.ec.europa.eu/en/library/data-act -proposal-regulation-harmonised-rules-fair-access-and-use-data.

32. European Data Protection Board and European Data Protection Supervisor, "EDPB-EDPS Joint Opinion 03/2021 on the Proposal for a Regulation of the European Parliament and of the European Council on European Data Governance (Data Governance Act)," March 10, 2021, 3.1(19), https://edpb.europa.eu/system /files/2021-03/edpb-edps_joint_opinion_dga_en.pdf.

33. See European Parliament, "Data Governance: Why Is the EU Data Sharing Law Important?," June 4, 2022, https://www.europarl.europa.eu/news/en/headlines /priorities/artificial-intelligence-in-the-eu/20220331STO26411/data-governance -why-is-the-eu-data-sharing-law-important.

34. See, for example, Timothy Ruff, "The Three Models of Digital Identity Relationships," *Medium*, April 24, 2018, https://medium.com/evernym/the-three-models-of -digital-identity-relationships-ca0727cb5186.

35. Massimo Ragnedda and Giuseppe Destefanis, ed., *Blockchain and Web 3.0: Social, Economic, and Technical Challenges* (Abingdon, UK: Routledge, 2021).

36. Phillip Windley, "How Blockchain Makes Self-Sovereign Identities Possible," *Computerworld*, January 10, 2018, https://www.computerworld.com/article/3244128 /how-blockchain-makes-self-sovereign-identities-possible.html.

37. https://solidproject.org.

38. Fabrice Coffrini, "Tim Berners-Lee's Plan to Save the Internet: Give Us Back Control of Our Data," *Conversation*, February 5, 2018, https://theconversation.com /tim-berners-lees-plan-to-save-the-internet-give-us-back-control-of-our-data-154130.

39. Heleen Janssen, Jennifer Cobbe, Chris Norval, and Jatinder Singh, "Decentralized Data Processing: Personal Data Stores and the GDPR," *International Data Privacy Law* 10, no. 4 (2020): 356–384, https://doi.org/10.1093/idpl/ipaa016.

40. Murat Sönmez, "How Data Exchanges Can Level the Digital Playing Field," World Economic Forum, June 28, 2019, https://www.weforum.org/agenda/2019 /06/data-exchanges-digital-ai-artificial-intelligence.

41. "About UBDI," digi.me, accessed April 18, 2022, https://digi.me/ubdi/#slide-0.

42. "Data Marketplaces with Blockchain Superpowers," Ocean Protocol, https://oceanprotocol.com/technology/marketplaces.

43. See "Data Marketplaces with Blockchain Superpowers," Ocean Protocol, accessed April 18, 2022, https://oceanprotocol.com/technology/marketplaces; https://data pace.io.

44. See, for example, Shiv Malik, "Steamr and Fysical to Partner to Reshape Human Location Data Market," *Medium*, May 1, 2018, https://medium.com/streamrblog /streamr-and-fysical-to-partner-to-reshape-human-location-data-market-e81ea80a7 e59; Jeanette Beebe, "You Can Now Make Money by Selling Your Own Health Data, but Should You?," *Fast Company*, September 27, 2019, https://www.fastcompany .com/90409942/would-you-sell-your-own-health-data-theres-a-market-for-it-but -ethical-concerns-remain; Will Douglas Heaven, "People Are Hiring out Their Faces to Become Deepfake-Style Marketing Clones," *MIT Technology Review*, August 27, 2021, https://www.technologyreview.com/2021/08/27/1033879/people-hiring-faces -work-deepfake-ai-marketing-clones.

45. See, for example, Luciano Floridi, *Information: A Very Short Introduction* (Oxford: Oxford University Press, 2010), 90.

46. Carissa Véliz, *Privacy Is Power: Why and How You Should Take Back Control of Your Data* (London: Melville House, 2021), 84.

47. Dipayan Ghosh, "Don't Give Up on Your Digital Privacy Yet," *Slate*, July 17, 2020, https://slate.com/technology/2020/07/data-privacy-surveillance-law-marketers .html.

48. Murat Sönmez, "How Personal Data Could Help Contribute to a COVID-19 Solution," World Economic Forum, March 23, 2020, https://www.weforum.org /agenda/2020/03/covid-19-personal-data-new-commodity-market/.

49. Chandra Steele, "How Much Is Your Personal Data Worth?," *PC Magazine*, November 25, 2020, https://www.pcmag.com/news/know-your-datas-worth.

50. Gregory Barber, "I Sold My Data for Crypto. Here's How Much I Made," *Wired*, December 17, 2018, https://www.wired.com/story/i-sold-my-data-for-crypto.

51. Casey Newton, "Facebook Has Been Paying Teens $20 a Month for Total Access to Their Phone Activity," *Verge*, January 29, 2019, https://www.theverge.com /2019/1/29/18202880/facebook-research-enterprise-root-certificate-onavo -techcrunch.

52. Zack Whittaker, "Amazon Will Pay You $10 in Credit for Your Palm Print Bio-metrics," *TechCrunch*, August 2, 2021, https://techcrunch.com/2021/08/02/amazon -credit-palm-biometrics; Mary Hanbury, "Amazon Is Offering People $25 Gift Cards

in Exchange for Taking 3D Scans of Their Bodies," *Business Insider*, May 23, 2019, https://www.businessinsider.com/amazon-offers-gift-cards-in-exchange-for-3d-body-scans-2019-5.

53. President's Council of Advisors on Science and Technology, *Big Data and Privacy: A Technological Perspective* (Washington, DC: Executive Office of the President, May 2014), https://obamawhitehouse.archives.gov/sites/default/files/microsites/ostp/PCAST/pcast_big_data_and_privacy_-_may_2014.pdf.

54. Woodrow Hartzog, *Privacy's Blueprint* (Cambridge, MA: Harvard University Press, 2018), 62–67.

55. Shoshana Zuboff, *The Age of Surveillance Capitalism: The Fight for a Human Future at the New Frontier of Power* (New York: Public Affairs, 2019), 94.

56. See generally Véliz, *Privacy Is Power*, 242.

57. Eric Posner and E. Glen Weyl, *Radical Markets* (Princeton, NJ: Princeton University Press, 2019).

58. Jack Hardinges, "Defining a 'Data Trust,'" Open Data Institute, October 19, 2018, https://theodi.org/article/defining-a-data-trust.

59. European Commission, "A European Strategy for Data."

60. See, for example, Jane R. Bambauer, "Tragedy of the Data Commons," *Harvard Journal of Law and Technology* 25 (March 19, 2011), https://ssrn.com/abstract=1789749.

Chapter 4

1. "Keynote Address from Tim Cook, CEO, Apple Inc.," YouTube, October 24, 2018, https://www.youtube.com/watch?v=kVhOLkIs20A.

2. "Privacy," Apple, https://www.apple.com/privacy. The App Tracking Transparency tool was rolled out as part of Apple's iOS 14.5 and has reportedly resulted in approximately 4 percent of users allowing tracking in the United States. See Rachel Kraus, "After Update, Only 4 Percent of iOS Users in U.S. Let Apps Track Them," *Mashable*, May 7, 2021, https://in.mashable.com/tech/22132/after-update-only-4-percent-of-ios-users-in-us-let-apps-track-them.

3. Hamza Shaban, "Apple Stars at Giant Tech Confab CES—without Actually being There," *Washington Post*, January 7, 2019, https://www.washingtonpost.com/technology/2019/01/07/apple-burns-google-giant-billboard-touting-privacy-ces.

4. Satya Nadella, "Privacy at Microsoft," accessed January 20, 2022, https://privacy.microsoft.com/en-us/.

5. Julie Brill, "Microsoft's Commitment to GDPR, Privacy and Putting Customers in Control of Their Own Data," Microsoft, May 21, 2018, https://blogs.microsoft.com /on-the-issues/2018/05/21/microsofts-commitment-to-gdpr-privacy-and-putting -customers-in-control-of-their-own-data.

6. Julie Brill, "Data Privacy: Consumers Want It, Businesses Need It—It's Time Our Government Delivers It," *Hill*, May 24, 2019, https://thehill.com/blogs/congress -blog/technology/445405-data-privacy-consumers-want-it-businesses-need-it-its -time-our.

7. Issie Lapowsky, "Microsoft Can't Get Its Privacy Bill Passed in Its Home State. It's Trying Its Luck Elsewhere," *Protocol*, April 28, 2020, https://www.protocol.com /microsoft-privacy-bills-in-four-other-states.

8. Mark Zuckerberg, "The Internet Needs New Rules. Let's Start in These Four Areas," *Washington Post*, March 30, 2019, https://www.washingtonpost.com/opinions/mark -zuckerberg-the-internet-needs-new-rules-lets-start-in-these-four-areas/2019/03/29 /9e6f0504-521a-11e9-a3f7-78b7525a8d5f_story.html.

9. Mark Zuckerberg, "The Internet Needs New Rules"; Alex Hern, "Facebook Moves 1.5bn Users Out of Reach of New European Privacy Law," *Guardian*, April 19, 2018, https://www.theguardian.com/technology/2018/apr/19/facebook-moves-15bn -users-out-of-reach-of-new-european-privacy-law.

10. Nick Statt, "Facebook CEO Mark Zuckerberg Says the 'Future Is Private,'" *Verge*, April 30, 2019, https://www.theverge.com/2019/4/30/18524188/facebook-f8-key note-mark-zuckerberg-privacy-future-2019.

11. See, for example, Patricio Robles, "Google Makes a Big Commitment in Its Pivot to Privacy: What Marketers Need to Know," Econsultancy, March 4, 2021, https:// econsultancy.com/google-makes-a-big-commitment-in-its-pivot-to-privacy-what -marketers-need-to-know.

12. Matthew Scott, "Google's Privacy Moves: Who Benefits?," *Digital Privacy News*, December 1, 2020, https://digitalprivacy.news/?p=6671.

13. Sundar Pichai, "Privacy Should Not Be a Luxury Good," *New York Times*, May 7, 2019, https://www.nytimes.com/2019/05/07/opinion/google-sundar-pichai-privacy .html.

14. See, for example, "Tech Companies Are Trying to Redefine Privacy—What's Missing Is Real Competition on Privacy," *Privacy International*, May 17, 2019, https://privacyinternational.org/long-read/2939/tech-companies-are-trying-redefine -privacy-whats-missing-real-competition-privacy.

15. See, for example, Mark Scott, "How Lobbyists Rewrote Washington State's Privacy Law," *Politico*, April 26, 2019, https://www.politico.eu/article/how-lobbyists -rewrote-washington-state-privacy-law-microsoft-amazon-regulation.

16. *Protecting Privacy in Practice: The Current Use, Development and Limits of Privacy Enhancing Technologies in Data Analysis* (London: Royal Society, March 2019), https://royalsociety.org/-/media/policy/projects/privacy-enhancing-technologies /privacy-enhancing-technologies-report.pdf.

17. "Protecting Data Privacy," Amazon, July 9, 2018, https://www.aboutamazon .com/news/amazon-ai/protecting-data-privacy.

18. Cynthia Dwork, "Differential Privacy," in *Automata, Languages and Programming*, ed. Michele Bugliesi, Bart Preneel, Vladimiro Sassone, and Ingo Wegener (New York: Springer, 2006), 1–12, https://doi.org/10.1007/11787006_1.

19. "Protecting Data Privacy."

20. See, for example, Dell Cameron, "A Very Long List of Privacy Features Google Talked about Today at Google I/O," *Gizmodo*, May 7, 2019, https://gizmodo.com /a-very-long-list-of-privacy-features-google-talked-abou-1834593900.

21. Justin Schuh, "Building a More Private Web," *Keyword* (blog), August 22, 2019, https://www.blog.google/products/chrome/building-a-more-private-web.

22. H. Brendan McMahan, Eider Moore, Daniel Ramage, Seth Hampton, and Blaise Agüera y Arcas, "Communication-Efficient Learning of Deep Networks from Decentralized Data," arxiv.org, February 28, 2017, https://arxiv.org/pdf/1602.05629.pdf.

23. See, for example, Mark Sullivan, "Google's Anti-Tracking Move Is Good for Privacy, and Even Better for Google," *Fast Company*, March 4, 2021, https://www .fastcompany.com/90610781/google-third-party-cookies-tracking-advertising.

24. Federica Laricchia, "Market Share of Mobile Operating Systems Worldwide 2012–2022," Statista, February 7, 2022, https://www.statista.com/statistics/272698 /global-market-share-held-by-mobile-operating-systems-since-2009.

25. Michael Kan, "Apple's Siri Can Now Process Many Requests without an Internet Connection," *PC Mag*, June 7, 2021, https://www.pcmag.com/news/apples-siri -can-now-process-many-requests-without-an-internet-connection.

26. Russell Brandom, "Android Introduces New Privacy-Friendly Sandbox for Machine Learning Data," *Verge*, May 18, 2021, https://www.theverge.com/2021/5 /18/22436367/google-io-android-private-computer-core-machine-learning-data -privacy.

27. Chris O'Brien, "Why IBM Believes Confidential Computing Is the Future of Cloud Security," *VentureBeat*, October 16, 2020, https://venturebeat.com/2020/10 /16/why-ibm-believes-confidential-computing-is-the-future-of-cloud-security.

28. Andreas Kopp, "Create Privacy-Preserving Synthetic Data for Machine Learning with SmartNoise," *Microsoft Open Source Blog*, February 18, 2021, https://cloudblogs

.microsoft.com/opensource/2021/02/18/create-privacy-preserving-synthetic-data
-for-machine-learning-with-smartnoise.

29. "Privacy-Enhancing Technologies: The Path to Anonymity, Volume 1," Information and Privacy Commissioner / Ontario Canada and Registratiekamer / The Netherlands (Report), August 1995, https://collections.ola.org/mon/10000/184530.pdf.

30. Privacy-enhancing computation and other PETs were also featured as top strategic technology trends for 2021 by Gartner. See Kasey Panetta, "Distributed Cloud, AI Engineering, Cybersecurity Mesh and Composable Business Drive Some of the Top Trends for 2021," Gartner, October 19, 2020, https://www.gartner.com/smarterwithgartner/gartner-top-strategic-technology-trends-for-2021.

31. Regulation (EU) 2016/679 of the European Parliament and European Council of April 27, 2016, on the protection of natural persons with regard to the processing of personal data and the free movement of such data, and repealing Directive 95/46/EC (General Data Protection Regulation), OJ 2016 L 119/1, Art. 25.

32. See, for example, "New Privacy Tech Industry Attracts Massive Funding," *Future of Privacy Forum*, July 11, 2019, https://fpf.org/blog/new-privacy-tech-industry-attracts-massive-funding.

33. Ian Goldberg, "Privacy-Enhancing Technologies for the Internet III: Ten Years Later," in *Digital Privacy: Theory, Technologies, and Practices*, ed. Alessandro Acquisti, Stefanos Grtizalis, Costas Lambrinoudakis, and Sabrina De Capitani di Vimercati (Boca Raton, FL: Auerbach Publications, 2008), 3–18.

34. *Protecting Privacy in Practice*.

35. See, for example, Data Protection Commission, *Report by the Data Protection Commission on the Use of Cookies and Other Tracking Technologies: Following a Sweep Conducted between August 2019 and December 2019*, April 6, 2020, https://www.dataprotection.ie/sites/default/files/uploads/2020-04/Report%20by%20the%20DPC%20on%20the%20use%20of%20cookies%20and%20other%20tracking%20technologies.pdf.

36. See, for example, William Stadler, "Risks of Privacy-Enhancing Technologies: Complexity and Implications of Differential Privacy in the Context of Cybercrime," in *Security and Privacy from a Legal, Ethical, and Technical Perspective*, ed. Christos Kalloniatis and Carlos Travieso-Gonzalez (Alphen aan den Rijn, Netherlands: Wolters Kluwer, 2020), 107–124.

37. See, for example, London Economics, *Study on the Economic Benefits of Privacy-Enhancing Technologies (PETs)*, July 2010, 8, https://londoneconomics.co.uk/wp-content/uploads/2011/09/17-Study-on-the-economic-benefits-of-privacy-enhancing-technologies-PETs.pdf.

38. Linux Foundation, "Confidential Computing Consortium: Defining and Enabling Confidential Computing," August 2018, https://confidentialcomputing.io /wp-content/uploads/sites/85/2019/12/CCC_Overview.pdf.

39. As privacy advocates caution, recalculating cohorts would actually keep user data fresh and make it easier to accurately track user behavior over time. Moreover, privacy would depend on the strength of the clustering algorithm and size of a cohort, putting minorities and marginalized individuals at heightened risk. See Bennett Cyphers, "Google's FLoC Is a Terrible Idea," Electronic Frontier Foundation, April 9, 2021, https://www.eff.org/deeplinks/2021/03/googles-floc-terrible-idea.

40. Cyphers, "Google's FLoC Is a Terrible Idea."

41. Issie Lapowsky, "FLoC Is Dead. But Topics Won't Fix Google's Ad Targeting Problems," *Protocol*, January 26, 2022, https://www.protocol.com/bulletins/floc -topics-google.

42. "Protecting Data Privacy."

43. See, for example, "Beginner's Guide to Federated Learning and Differential Privacy," MMA, March 27, 2020, https://www.mmaglobal.com/articles/beginners -guide-federated-learning-differential-privacy.

44. Neal Cohen, *The Ethical Use of Personal Data to Build AI Technologies* (Cambridge, MA: Carr Center for Human Rights Policy at Harvard Kennedy School, 2020), https://carrcenter.hks.harvard.edu/files/cchr/files/200228_ccdp_neal_cohen.pdf.

45. Datagen, "Our Technology," accessed April 19, 2022, https://www.datagen .tech.

46. Karen Hao, "These Creepy Fake Humans Herald a New Age in AI," *MIT Technology Review*, June 11, 2021, https://www.technologyreview.com/2021/06/11/1026135 /ai-synthetic-data.

47. For example, to generate synthetic people, synthetic data company Datagen first scans actual humans. Hao, "These Creepy Fake Humans."

48. See generally Merel Koning, Paulan Korenhof, Gergely Alpar, and Jaap-Henk Hoepman, "The ABC of ABC: An Analysis of Attribute-Based Credentials in the Light of Data Protection, Privacy, and Identity," *Internet, Law and Politics: A Decade of Transformations* 10, no. 1 (2014): 357–374, http://www.cs.ru.nl/~gergely/objects /ABCs_IDP.pdf.

49. Michael Veale, "Privacy Is Not the Problem with the Apple-Google Contact-Tracing Toolkit," *Guardian*, July 1, 2020, https://www.theguardian.com/commentis free/2020/jul/01/apple-google-contact-tracing-app-tech-giant-digital-rights.

50. See, for example, Luc Rocher, Julien M. Hendrickx, and Yves-Alexandre de Montjoye, "Estimating the Success of Re-Identifications in Incomplete Datasets

Using Generative Models," *Nature Communications* 10 (2019), https://doi.org/10.1038/s41467-019-10933-3; Paul M. Schwartz and Daniel J. Solove, "The PII Problem: Privacy and a New Concept of Personally Identifiable Information," *New York University Law Review* 86, no. 6 (December 2011): 1814–1894; Paul Ohm, "Broken Promises of Privacy: Responding to the Surprising Failure of Anonymization," *UCLA Law Review* 57 (2010): 1701–1777.

51. Zack Whittaker, "How Strava's 'Anonymized' Fitness Tracking Data Spilled Government Secrets," *ZDNet*, January 29, 2018, https://www.zdnet.com/article/strava-anonymized-fitness-tracking-data-government-opsec.

52. Nick Statt, "Facebook CEO Mark Zuckerberg Says the 'Future Is Private,'" *The Verge*, April 30, 2019, https://www.theverge.com/2019/4/30/18524188/facebook-f8-keynote-mark-zuckerberg-privacy-future-2019.

53. Geoffrey A. Fowler, "It's the Middle of the Night. Do You Know Who Your iPhone Is Talking to?," *Washington Post*, May 28, 2019, https://www.washingtonpost.com/technology/2019/05/28/its-middle-night-do-you-know-who-your-iphone-is-talking.

54. See, for example, Matthew Scott, "Google's Privacy Moves: Who Benefits?," *Digital Privacy News*, December 1, 2020, https://digitalprivacy.news/?p=6671.

55. Alongside the Privacy Sandbox, Google announced a host of other changes in the name of user privacy, including updated settings and controls for its Google Analytics products, adjustments to its API permissions to block certain third-party browser extensions, and the discontinuation of its emergency location-sharing app based on a list of trusted contacts. On closer examination, many of the changes were not as privacy enhancing as advertised by Google. The changes to Google Analytics gave advertisers expanded AI and machine learning–powered insights, deeper integration with Google Ads, and better cross-device measurement capabilities. The API tweaks designed to block third-party browser extensions would give Google the discretion to classify certain ad blockers and other proprivacy extensions as *malicious*. And by ending emergency location sharing with a small list of trusted contacts, Google users would be redirected to broadcast their location data via Google Maps. See, for example, Elizabeth M. Renieris, "What Google's Privacy Sandbox Means for Internet Governance," Centre for International Governance Innovation, March 19, 2021, https://www.cigionline.org/articles/what-googles-privacy-sandbox-means-internet-governance.

56. Justin Schuh, "Building a More Private Web," *Keyword* (blog), August 22, 2019, https://www.blog.google/products/chrome/building-a-more-private-web.

57. See Michael Grothaus, "Exclusive: Apple's Craig Federighi on WWDC's New Privacy Features," *Fast Company*, June 7, 2021, https://www.fastcompany.com/90643627/apple-privacy-wwdc-private-relay-vpn-icloud-plus-macos-monterey.

58. See, for example, Mark Scott, "Apple Stands in the Global Antitrust Crosshairs," *Politico*, August 7, 2019, https://www.politico.com/story/2019/08/07/apple-antitrust-europe-united-states-1449919.

59. Apple and Google, "Exposure Notification Privacy-Preserving Analytics (ENPA) White Paper," April 2021, https://covid19-static.cdn-apple.com/applications/covid19/current/static/contact-tracing/pdf/ENPA_White_Paper.pdf.

60. Apple and Google, "Exposure Notifications: Frequently Asked Questions," September 2020, https://covid19-static.cdn-apple.com/applications/covid19/current/static/contact-tracing/pdf/ExposureNotification-FAQv1.2.pdf.

61. See, for example, David Meyer, "Apple and Google Flex Privacy Muscles with Blockage of English COVID Contact-Tracing App Update," *Fortune*, April 12, 2021, https://fortune.com/2021/04/12/apple-google-block-covid-contact-tracing-app-england-wales.

62. Natasha Singer, "Why Apple and Google's Virus Alert Apps Had Limited Success," *New York Times*, May 27, 2021, https://www.nytimes.com/2021/05/27/business/apple-google-virus-tracing-app.html.

63. For example, when European Union president Ursula von der Leyen initially announced Europe's version, she first and foremost asserted that it would "respect data protection, security [and] privacy." Ursula von der Leyen, tweet, March 1, 2021, https://twitter.com/vonderleyen/status/1366346729289904128?s=20.

64. See, for example, Elizabeth M. Renieris, "What's Really at Stake with Vaccine Passports," Centre for International Governance Innovation, April 5, 2021, https://www.cigionline.org/articles/whats-really-stake-vaccine-passports.

Chapter 5

1. Accenture, *The Post-Digital Era Is upon Us: Are You Ready for What's Next?* (Dublin: Accenture, 2019), 2, 12, https://www.accenture.com/t20190201T224653Z__w__/us-en/_acnmedia/PDF-94/Accenture-TechVision-2019-Tech-Trends-Report.pdf#zoom=50.

2. Access Now, "Dear Spotify: Don't Manipulate Our Emotions for Profit," May 4, 2021, https://www.accessnow.org/spotify-tech-emotion-manipulation.

3. Umberto Bacchi, "Spotify Urged to Rule Out 'Invasive' Voice Recognition Tech," Reuters, May 4, 2021, https://www.reuters.com/article/us-tech-music-privacy/spotify-urged-to-rule-out-invasive-voice-recognition-tech-idUSKBN2CL1K9.

4. Access Now, "Dear Spotify."

5. Adam Tanner, "Can Technology Read Your Emotions?," *Consumer Reports*, August 2, 2021, https://www.consumerreports.org/artificial-intelligence/can-tech nology-read-your-emotions-a1096874808.

6. Article 19, *Emotional Entanglement: China's Emotion Recognition Market and Its Implications for Human Rights* (London: Article 19, January 2021), https://www .article19.org/wp-content/uploads/2021/01/ER-Tech-China-Report.pdf.

7. See, for example, Mike Elgan, "What Happens When Cars Get Emotional?," *Fast Company*, June 27, 2019, https://www.fastcompany.com/90368804/emotion -sensing-cars-promise-to-make-our-roads-much-safer.

8. Milly Chan, "This AI Reads Children's Emotions as They Learn," CNN, February 17, 2021, https://www.cnn.com/2021/02/16/tech/emotion-recognition-ai-education -spc-intl-hnk/index.html; Article 19, *Emotional Entanglement*.

9. IEEE Brain, "Future Neural Therapeutics: Technology Roadmap White Paper Version 2," IEEE, December 2020, https://brain.ieee.org/wp-content/uploads/2021/05 /Future-Neural-Therapeutics-WP-V2.1.pdf.

10. "Neurotechnology Market to Reach USD 19 Billion by 2026," *Medgadget*, March 9, 2020, https://www.medgadget.com/2020/03/neurotechnology-market-to-reach-usd -19-billion-by-2026-cisco-systems-inc-bmc-software-inc-abb-limited-dell-inc-fujitsu -ltd.html.

11. "Deep Brain Stimulation (DBS) for the Treatment of Parkinson's Disease and Other Movement Disorders," National Institute of Neurological Disorders and Stroke, accessed April 20, 2022, https://www.ninds.nih.gov/About-NINDS/Impact /NINDS-Contributions-Approved-Therapies/DBS.

12. Jonathan M. Gitlin, "Project SAM Gave a Paralyzed Racer His Wheels Back— and He Took Us for a Spin," *Ars Technica*, August 28, 2017, https://arstechnica.com /cars/2017/08/project-sam-gave-a-paralyzed-racer-his-wheels-back-and-he-took-us -for-a-spin.

13. Adi Robertson, "Facebook Shows Off How You'll Use Its Neural Wristbands with AR Glasses," *Verge*, March 18, 2021, https://www.theverge.com/2021/3/18 /22338008/facebook-reality-labs-emg-wristbands-ctrl-labs-ar-interface-demo.

14. See Sarah McBride, "NYC Brain Computer Startup Announces FDA Trial before Elon Musk," *Bloomberg*, July 28, 2021, https://www.bloomberg.com/news/articles /2021-07-28/elon-musk-neuralink-competitor-announces-fda-trial-for-brain-device.

15. Rafael Yuste, Jared Genser, and Stephanie Herrmann, "It's Time for Neuro-Rights: New Human Rights for the Age of Neurotechnology," *Horizons*, no. 18 (Winter 2021): 154–164, https://www.cirsd.org/files/000/000/008/47/7dc9d3b6165 ee497761b0abe69612108833b5cff.pdf.

16. See, for example, Eben Harrell, "Neuromarketing: What You Need to Know," *Harvard Business Review*, January 23, 2019, https://hbr.org/2019/01/neuromarketing-what-you-need-to-know.

17. Knud Lasse Lueth, "State of the IoT 2020: 12 Billion IoT Connections, Surpassing Non-IoT for the First Time," IoT Analytics, November 19, 2020, https://iot-analytics.com/state-of-the-iot-2020-12-billion-iot-connections-surpassing-non-iot-for-the-first-time.

18. See, for example, Ashley Carman, "Can a Bluetooth-Enabled Pill Help You Remember Your Medicine?," *Verge*, May 2, 2017, https://www.theverge.com/circuit breaker/2017/5/2/15507102/smart-pill-cap-pillsy-launch.

19. See, for example, Marshall Allen, "You Snooze, You Lose: Insurers Make the Old Adage Literally True," *Ars Technica*, November 21, 2018, https://arstechnica.com/science/2018/11/you-snooze-you-lose-insurers-make-the-old-adage-literally-true.

20. See, for example, Payal Dhar, "Study: 6G's Haptic, Holographic Future? Possibilities and Challenges for Future 6G Communications Networks," *IEEE Spectrum*, June 24, 2021, https://spectrum.ieee.org/6g-haptic-holography.

21. Satish Rupraoji Billewar, Karuna Jadhav, V. P. Sriram, A. Arun, Sikandar Mohd Abdul, Kamal Gulati, and Narinder Kumar Bhasin, "The Rise of 3D e-Commerce: The Online Shopping Gets Real with Virtual Reality and Augmented Reality during COVID-19," *World Journal of Engineering*, September 23, 2021, https://doi.org/10.1108/WJE-06-2021-0338.

22. See, for example, Tara L. Jeffs, "Virtual Reality and Special Needs," special issue, *Themes in Science and Technology Education* (2009): 253–268, https://files.eric.ed.gov/fulltext/EJ1131319.pdf.

23. "Where Do You Want to Go Today?," Google Arts and Culture, accessed April 20, 2022, https://artsandculture.google.com/project/expeditions.

24. Joseph Jerome and Jeremy Greenberg, "Augmented Reality and Virtual Reality: Privacy and Autonomy Considerations in Emerging, Immersive Digital Worlds," *Future of Privacy Forum*, April 2021, 13, https://fpf.org/wp-content/uploads/2021/04/FPF-ARVR-Report-4.16.21-Digital.pdf.

25. Lucas Matney and Taylor Hatmaker, "Zuckerberg Is Turning Trillion-Dollar Facebook into a 'Metaverse' Company, He Tells Investors," *TechCrunch*, July 28, 2021, https://techcrunch.com/2021/07/28/zuckerberg-is-turning-trillion-dollar-facebook-into-a-metaverse-company-he-tells-investors.

26. "Extended Reality (XR) Market Size to Reach USD 393 Billion by 2025 at 69.4% CAGR—Report by Market Research Future (MRFR)," *Intrado Globenewsire*, August 9, 2021, https://www.globenewswire.com/en/news-release/2021/08/09/2277296/0/en

/Extended-Reality-XR-Market-Size-to-Reach-USD-393-Billion-by-2025-at-69-4-CAGR
-Report-by-Market-Research-Future-MRFR.html.

27. Laurence Goasduff, "Key Priorities for IAM Leaders in 2021," Gartner, March 16, 2021, https://www.gartner.com/smarterwithgartner/key-priorities-for-iam-leaders -in-2021.

28. See Kevin Wack, "Contactless Payments: The Future Is Here," *American Banker*, June 23, 2020, https://www.americanbanker.com/news/contactless-payments-the -future-is-here.

29. See, for example, Ashley Wong, "Vaccine Mandate for Indoor Venues Starts in New York City," *New York Times*, August 17, 2021, https://www.nytimes.com/2021 /08/17/nyregion/vaccine-mandate-indoor-venues.html; Danielle Abril, "As Delta Variant Spreads, Some Companies with Vaccine Mandates Deploy Tech to Verify Records," *Washington Post*, August 19, 2021, https://www.washingtonpost.com /technology/2021/08/19/employers-vaccine-mandate-status-verification.

30. Elizabeth M. Renieris, "Identity in a 'Phygital' World: Why the Shift to Machine-Readable Humans Demands Better Digital ID Governance," Centre for International Governance Innovation, August 16, 2021, https://www.cigionline.org /articles/identity-in-a-phygital-world-why-the-shift-to-machine-readable-humans -demands-better-digital-id-governance.

31. See, for example, Ramaswamy Palaniappan, "Two-Stage Biometric Authentica- tion Method Using Thought Activity Brain Waves," *International Journal of Neural Systems* 18, no. 1 (2008): 59–66, https://www.worldscientific.com/doi/10.1142 /S0129065708001373.

32. Neal Cohen, "The Ethical Use of Personal Data to Build AI Technologies: A Case Study on Remote Biometric Identity Verification," Harvard Carr Center for Human Rights Policy, April 2020, https://carrcenter.hks.harvard.edu/files/cchr/files /200228_ccdp_neal_cohen.pdf.

33. See, for example, Luana Pascu, "Behavioral Biometrics and Persona-Based Secu- rity Intelligence as a Key Fraud Prevention Layer," *Biometric Update*, February 6, 2020, https://www.biometricupdate.com/202002/behavioral-biometrics-and-persona -based-security-intelligence-as-a-key-fraud-prevention-layer.

34. "Smart Cities and Inclusive Growth," Organisation for Economic Co-operation and Development, 2020, 8, 9, https://www.oecd.org/cfe/cities/OECD_Policy_Paper _Smart_Cities_and_Inclusive_Growth.pdf.

35. Linnet Taylor, Christine Richter, Shazade Jameson, and Carmen Perez de Pulgar, "Customers, Users or Citizens? Inclusion, Spatial Data and Governance in the Smart City," Maps4Society, June 9, 2016, http://ssrn.com/abstract=2792565.

36. Ben Green, *The Smart Enough City* (Cambridge, MA: MIT Press, 2019), 98.

37. See, for example, Pratibha Vuppuluri, "Investing in Innovation: The Rise of the Smart City," *Forbes*, December 3, 2020, https://www.forbes.com/sites/forbesfinance council/2020/12/03/investing-in-innovation-the-rise-of-the-smart-city/?sh=6229 c5915ba6.

38. See, for example, Stephanie Kanowitz, "Pandemic Accelerated Rise of Smart Cities," *GCN*, April 1, 2021, https://gcn.com/articles/2021/04/01/pandemic-acceler ated-smart-cities.aspx.

39. Green, *The Smart Enough City*, 100–103.

40. Laura DeNardis, *The Internet in Everything: Freedom and Security in a World with No Off Switch* (New Haven, CT: Yale University Press, 2020), 157.

41. Mireille Hildebrandt, *Smart Technologies and the End(s) of Law* (Cheltenham, UK: Edward Elgar Publishing, 2015), 40.

42. Julie E. Cohen, "The Emergent Limbic Media System," in *Life and Law in the Era of Data-Driven Agency*, ed. Mireille Hildebrandt and Kieron O'Hara (Cheltenham, UK: Edward Elgar, 2020), 60–79.

43. Stacey Higginbotham, "Reckoning with Tech before It Becomes Invisible: Facial Recognition, Route-Finding Software, and More Have the Potential for Dire Consequences," *IEEE Spectrum*, June 25, 2021, https://spectrum.ieee.org/reckoning -with-tech-before-it-becomes-invisible#toggle-gdpr.

44. Shoshana Zuboff, *The Age of Surveillance Capitalism: The Fight for a Human Future at the New Frontier of Power* (New York: Public Affairs, 2019), 482.

45. Zak Doffman, "Black Lives Matter: U.S. Protestors Tracked by Secretive Phone Location Technology," *Forbes*, June 26, 2020, https://www.forbes.com/sites/zakdoff man/2020/06/26/secretive-phone-tracking-company-publishes-location-data-on -black-lives-matter-protesters/?sh=40f2839d4a1e.

46. Jonathan Herring and Jesse Wall, "The Nature and Significance of the Right to Bodily Integrity," *Cambridge Law Journal* 76, no. 3 (November 2017): 566–588, https://doi.org/10.1017/S0008197317000605.

47. Restatement (Second) of Torts, § 652 (1977).

48. Jerome and Greenberg, "Augmented Reality."

49. Julia Keseru, "Bodies of Data or 'Databodies'?," *Medium* (blog), January 26, 2022, https://jkeserue.medium.com/bodies-of-data-or-databodies-608cce562d65.

50. Karl Ricanek and Benjamin Barbour, "What Are Soft Biometrics and How Can They Be Used?," *Computer* 44, no. 9 (September 12, 2011): 106–108, https://ieeex plore.ieee.org/document/6017182.

51. European Data Protection Supervisor, "Towards a New Digital Ethics: Data, Dignity and Technology," Opinion 4/2015, September 11, 2015, https://edps.europa.eu/sites/edp/files/publication/15-09-11_data_ethics_en.pdf.

52. For example, the CCPA's requirements do not apply to "consumer information that is deidentified or in the aggregate." See CCPA, § 1798.145(a)(5).

53. Alicia Solow-Niederman, "Information Privacy and the Inference Economy," SSRN Scholarly Paper (Rochester, NY: Social Science Research Network, September 10, 2021), https://papers.ssrn.com/abstract=3921003.

54. See, e.g., Sandra Wachter and Brent Mittelstadt, "A Right To Reasonable Inferences Re-Thinking Data Protection Law In The Age Of Big Data And AI," *Columbia Business Law Review* 2 (2019): 5-6, https://papers.ssrn.com/sol3/papers.cfm?abstract_id=3248829.

55. Andrew McStay, "Emotional AI, Soft Biometrics and the Surveillance of Emotional Life: An Unusual Consensus on Privacy," *Big Data and Society*, January 2020, https://doi.org/10.1177/2053951720904386.

56. Andrew McStay, "The Right to Privacy in the Age of Emotional AI," OCHR Report, 8, https://www.ohchr.org/Documents/Issues/DigitalAge/ReportPrivacyinDigital Age/AndrewMcStayProfessor%20of%20Digital%20Life,%20BangorUniversity WalesUK.pdf.

Chapter 6

1. Daniel Ackerman, "Before Face Masks, Americans Went to War against Seat Belts," *Business Insider*, May 26, 2020, https://www.businessinsider.com/when-amer icans-went-to-war-against-seat-belts-2020-5.

2. See "Census Questionnaire Content, 1990 CQC-26," Bureau of the Census, accessed April 21, 2022, https://www2.census.gov/library/publications/decennial /1990/cqc/cqc-26.pdf.

3. Ralph Nader, *Unsafe at Any Speed: The Designed-In Dangers of the American Automobile* (New York: Grossman Publishers, 1965).

4. See, for example, "Technology Sector," Morningstar, accessed January 5, 2022, https://www.morningstar.com/InvGlossary/technology_sector.aspx.

5. Merritt Roe Smith and Leo Marx, *Does Technology Drive History? The Dilemma of Technological Determinism* (Cambridge, MA: MIT Press, 1994).

6. See, for example, European Commission "Europe Fit for the Digital Age: Commission Proposes New Rules for Digital Platforms," press release, December 15, 2020, https://ec.europa.eu/commission/presscorner/detail/en/ip_20_2347.

7. James Swann, "Your Fitbit Steps May Not Be Protected under Federal Law," *Bloomberg Law*, May 30, 2018, https://news.bloomberglaw.com/pharma-and-life-sciences/video-your-fitbit-steps-may-not-be-protected-by-federal-law?context=search&index=3.

8. See, for example, Kate Patrick, "Unregulated Fintech Could Be the Source of the Next Market Crash," *Inside Sources*, September 24, 2018, https://insidesources.com/unregulated-fintech-market-crash-algorithm-lending-great-recession-financial-crisis.

9. Kenneth Cukier and Viktor Mayer-Schönberger, *Big Data: A Revolution That Will Transform How We Live, Work, and Think* (Boston: Houghton Mifflin Harcourt, 2013), chap. 5.

10. Nick Couldry and Ulises A. Mejias, "Datafication," *Internet Policy Review* 8, no. 4 (November 2019), https://doi.org/10.14763/2019.4.1428.

11. José van Dijck, "Datafication, Dataism and Dataveillance: Big Data between Scientific Paradigm and Ideology," *Surveillance and Society* 12, no. 2 (2014), 197–208, https://doi.org/10.24908/ss.v12i2.4776.

12. Nicholas Negroponte, *Being Digital* (New York: Knopf, 1995), 4.

13. Mireille Hildebrandt, *Smart Technologies and the End(s) of Law* (Cheltenham, UK: Edward Elgar Publishing, 2015), 43–44.

14. Kate Crawford, *Atlas of AI: Power, Politics, and the Planetary Costs of Artificial Intelligence* (New Haven, CT: Yale University Press, 2021), 113.

15. Hildebrandt, *Smart Technologies*, 44–45.

16. Shoshana Zuboff, *The Age of Surveillance Capitalism: The Fight for a Human Future at the New Frontier of Power* (New York: Public Affairs, 2019), 233–235, 290.

17. Nick Couldry and Ulises A. Mejias, *The Costs of Connection: How Data Is Colonizing Human Life and Appropriating It for Capitalism* (Redwood City, CA: Stanford University Press, 2019), 17.

18. See, for example, Stu Woo, "Facebook Backs Underwater Cable Projects to Boost Internet Connectivity," *Wall Street Journal*, August 16, 2021, https://www.wsj.com/articles/facebook-backs-underwater-cable-projects-to-boost-internet-connectivity-11629127381.

19. Crawford, *Atlas of AI*, 93.

20. See Regulation (EU) 2016/679 of the European Parliament and European Council of April 27, 2016, on the protection of natural persons with regard to the processing of personal data and the free movement of such data, and repealing Directive 95/46/EC (General Data Protection Regulation), OJ 2016 L 119/1, Art. 5(b)–(c).

21. California Privacy Rights and Enforcement Act of 2020, amendments to version 3, November 4, 2019, § 1798.100(c), https://oag.ca.gov/system/files/initiatives/pdfs/19-0021A1%20%28Consumer%20Privacy%20-%20Version%203%29_1.pdf.

22. See, for example, Huaxin Li, Qingrong Chen, Haojin Zhu, Di Ma, Hong Wen, and Xuemin Sherman Shen, "Privacy Leakage via De-Anonymization and Aggregation in Heterogeneous Social Networks," *IEEE Transactions on Dependable and Secure Computing* 17, no. 2 (March–April 2020): 350–362, https://www.computer.org/csdl/journal/tq/2020/02/08047477/13rRUEgs2uJ.

23. Couldry and Mejias, *The Costs of Connection*, 164.

24. See Lisa Feldman Barrett, Ralph Adolphs, Stacy Marsella, Aleix M. Martinez, and Seth D. Pollak, "Emotional Expressions Reconsidered: Challenges to Inferring Emotion from Human Facial Movements." *Psychological Science in the Public Interest* 20, no. 1 (July 2019): 1–68, https://doi.org/10.1177/1529100619832930.

25. See, for example, Evan Selinger, "A.I. Can't Detect Our Emotions," *One Zero*, April 6, 2021, https://onezero.medium.com/a-i-cant-detect-our-emotions-3c1f6fce2539.

26. See, for example, Sianne Ngai, "'A Foul Lump Started Making Promises in My Voice': Race, Affect, and the Animated Subject," *American Literature* 74, no. 3 (2002): 571–601, https://muse.jhu.edu/article/1850.

27. See, for example, Lauren Rhue, "Racial Influence on Automated Perceptions of Emotions," *Race, AI, and Emotions* (November 9, 2018), http://dx.doi.org/10.2139/ssrn.3281765.

28. Artem Domnich and Gholamreza Anbarjafari, "Responsible AI: Gender Bias Assessment in Emotion Recognition," ArXiv abs/2103.11436, March 21, 2021, https://arxiv.org/abs/2103.11436.

29. Liam Drew, "The Ethics of Brain-Computer Interfaces," *Nature*, July 24, 2019, https://www.nature.com/articles/d41586-019-02214-2?proof=t%25C2%25A0; Arthur P. Shimamura, "Bridging Psychological and Biological Science: The Good, Bad, and Ugly," *Perspectives on Psychological Science* 5, no. 6 (2010): 772–775, http://www.jstor.org/stable/41613596.

30. Stephen Rainey, Stéphanie Martin, Andy Christen, Pierre Mégevand, and Eric Fourneret, "Brain Recording, Mind-Reading, and Neurotechnology: Ethical Issues from Consumer Devices to Brain-Based Speech Decoding," *Science and Engineering Ethics* 26 (2020): 2295–2311, https://doi.org/10.1007/s11948-020-00218-0.

31. Drew, "The Ethics of Brain-Computer Interfaces."

32. See, for example, Rainey et al., "Brain Recording."

33. See, for example, Sjors Ligthart, Thomas Douglas, Christoph Bublitz, Tijs Kooijmans, and Gerben Meynen, "Forensic Brain-Reading and Mental Privacy in European Human Rights Law: Foundations and Challenges," *Neuroethics* 14 (June 2020): 191–203, https://doi.org/10.1007/s12152-020-09438-4.

34. Sun-Ha Hong, *Technologies of Speculation: The Limits of Knowledge in a Data-Driven Society* (New York: NYU Press, 2020), 21, 23–24.

35. "The Precautionary Principle," World Commission on the Ethics of Scientific Knowledge and Technology, March 2005, https://unesdoc.unesco.org/ark:/48223 /pf0000139578.

36. Susie Alegre, "Rethinking Freedom of Thought for the 21st Century," *European Human Rights Law Review* 3 (2017): 221–233, https://doi.org/10.13140/RG.2.2 .27905.07529.

37. Zuboff, *The Age of Surveillance Capitalism*, 92–94.

38. Andrew McStay, "The Right to Privacy in the Age of Emotional AI," OCHR Report, 4, https://www.ohchr.org/Documents/Issues/DigitalAge/ReportPrivacyinDigital Age/AndrewMcStayProfessor%20of%20Digital%20Life,%20BangorUniversityWales UK.pdf.

39. Couldry and Mejias, *The Costs of Connection*, 172–173.

40. Michael Sandel, *What Money Can't Buy: The Moral Limits of Markets* (New York: Farrar, Straus and Giroux, 2013), 130.

41. Sandel, *What Money Can't Buy*, 8–9, 202–203.

42. Couldry and Mejias, *The Costs of Connection*, 180–181.

43. Carissa Véliz, *Privacy Is Power: Why and How You Should Take Back Control of Your Data* (London: Melville House, 2021), 87, 109.

44. Michael Veale, "Privacy Is Not the Problem with the Apple-Google Contact-Tracing Toolkit," *Guardian*, July 1, 2020, https://www.theguardian.com/commentis free/2020/jul/01/apple-google-contact-tracing-app-tech-giant-digital-rights.

45. Véliz, *Privacy Is Power*, 109.

46. Zuboff, *The Age of Surveillance Capitalism*, 11, 105.

47. Kate Crawford, Roel Dobbe, Theodora Dryer, Genevieve Fried, Ben Green, Elizabeth Kaziunas, Amba Kak, et al., *AI Now 2019 Report* (New York: AI Now Institute, 2019), 6, https://ainowinstitute.org/AI_Now_2019_Report.html.

48. Jonathan Greig, "One Year after Amazon, Microsoft and IBM Ended Facial Recognition Sales to Police, Smaller Players Fill Void," *ZDNet*, May 26, 2021, https://

www.zdnet.com/article/one-year-after-amazon-microsoft-and-ibm-ended-facial-recognition-sales-to-police-smaller-players-fill-void.

49. Crawford, *Atlas of AI*, 120–121.

50. Couldry and Mejias, *The Costs of Connection*, 41.

51. See Citizens United v. Federal Election Commission, 558 U.S. 310 (2010).

52. Kashmir Hill, "Facial Recognition Start-up Mounts a First Amendment Defense," *New York Times*, August 11, 2020, https://www.nytimes.com/2020/08/11/technology/clearview-floyd-abrams.html?.

53. Rebecca MacKinnon, *Consent of the Networked: The Worldwide Struggle for Internet Freedom* (New York: Basic Books, 2012).

54. See, for example, Naomi Klein, "Screen New Deal," *Intercept*, May 8, 2020, https://theintercept.com/2020/05/08/andrew-cuomo-eric-schmidt-coronavirus-tech-shock-doctrine.

Chapter 7

1. See, for example, "2020 Ranking Digital Rights Corporate Accountability Index Research Indicators," Ranking Digital Rights, accessed February 14, 2022, https://rankingdigitalrights.org/index2020/methodology. ("Indicators in this category seek evidence that the company has governance processes in place to ensure that it respects the human rights to freedom of expression and privacy.")

2. Article 19, https://www.article19.org.

3. As the signatories to the International Bill of Human Rights acknowledged, "The ideal of free human beings enjoying freedom from fear and want can only be achieved if conditions are created whereby everyone may enjoy his economic, social and cultural rights, as well as his civil and political rights." See UN General Assembly, International Covenant on Economic, Social and Cultural Rights, International Covenant on Civil and Political Rights and Optional Protocol to the International Covenant on Civil and Political Rights, December 16, 1966, A/RES/2200, "Preamble," https://www.ohchr.org/en/professionalinterest/pages/cescr.aspx (hereafter ICESCR).

4. John Perry Barlow, "A Declaration of the Independence of Cyberspace," Electronic Frontier Foundation, February 8, 1996, https://www.eff.org/cyberspace-independence.

5. ICESCR, Art. 6–15. ESCRs are also enshrined in various regional human rights instruments, such as the European Convention for the Protection of Human Rights and Fundamental Freedoms, American Convention on Human Rights, and African Charter on Human and Peoples' Rights.

6. See, for example, John Humphrey, "The International Law of Human Rights in the Middle Twentieth Century," Present State of International Law and Other Essays Written in Honor of the Centenary Celebration of the International Law Association 75 (London: International Law Association, 1973), https://www.tjsl.edu /slomansonb/10.1_HRMid20.pdf. ("The principal characteristic of the twentieth century approach to human rights has been its unambiguous recognition of the fact that all human beings are entitled to the enjoyment not only of the traditional civil and political rights but also the economic, social and cultural rights without which, for most people, the traditional rights have little meaning.")

7. See ICESCR, Art. 2.1. ("Each State Party to the present Covenant undertakes to take steps, individually and through international assistance and co-operation, especially economic and technical, to the maximum of its available resources, with a view to achieving progressively the full realization of the rights recognized in the present Covenant by all appropriate means, including particularly the adoption of legislative measures.")

8. See, for example, "Fact Sheet No. 33: Frequently Asked Questions on Economic, Social and Cultural Rights," UN Office of the High Commissioner for Human Rights, December 1, 2008, https://www.ohchr.org/en/publications/fact-sheets/fact -sheet-no-33-frequently-asked-questions-economic-social-and-cultural.

9. "Fact Sheet No. 33," 9.

10. See, for example, Stephen Holmes and Cass Sunstein, *The Cost of Rights: Why Liberty Depends on Taxes* (New York: W. W. Norton, 1999).

11. See, for example, Michelle Bachelet, "Human Rights in the Digital Age—Can They Make a Difference?," UN Office of the High Commissioner for Human Rights, October 17, 2019, https://www.ohchr.org/en/NewsEvents/Pages/DisplayNews.aspx ?NewsID=25158&LangID=E.

12. See, for example, Kate Klonick, "The New Governors: The People, Rules, and Processes Governing Online Speech," *Harvard Law Review* 131 (2018): 1618–1625, https://harvardlawreview.org/2018/04/the-new-governors-the-people-rules-and -processes-governing-online-speech.

13. See, for example, "2020 Ranking Digital Rights Corporate Accountability Index Indicators."

14. See Joseph Jerome and Jeremy Greenberg, "Augmented Reality and Virtual Reality: Privacy and Autonomy Considerations in Emerging, Immersive Digital Worlds," *Future of Privacy Forum*, April 2021, 24, https://fpf.org/wp-content/uploads/2021/04 /FPF-ARVR-Report-4.16.21-Digital.pdf.

15. See Katitza Rodriguez and Kurt Opsahl, "Augmented Reality Must Have Augmented Privacy," Electronic Frontier Foundation, October 16, 2020, https://www .eff.org/deeplinks/2020/10/augmented-reality-must-have-augmented-privacy.

16. See generally Eli Pariser, *The Filter Bubble: How the New Personalized Web Is Changing What We Read and How We Think* (London: Penguin Books, 2012).

17. See, for example, Julie Carr Smyth, "States Push Back against Use of Facial Recognition by Police," ABC News, May 5, 2021, https://abcnews.go.com/Politics/wireStory/states-push-back-facial-recognition-police-77510175.

18. See International Covenant on Civil and Political Rights, December 19, 1966, 999 UNTS 171, Can TS 1976 No. 47 (entered into force on March 23, 1976), Art. 18(1)–(2) (hereafter ICCPR). ("Everyone shall have the right to freedom of thought, conscience and religion," "No one shall be subject to coercion which would impair his freedom to have or to adopt a religion or belief of his choice.") Similarly, Articles 9 and 10 of the European Convention on Human Rights stipulate, respectively, that "everyone has the right to freedom of thought, conscience and religion" along with the "freedom to hold opinions . . . without interference by public authority and regardless of frontiers." In the United States, courts have recognized a First Amendment right to the freedom of thought as necessary for free speech and expression. See, for example, *Ashcroft v. Free Speech Coalition*, 535 U.S. 234 at 253, 122 S. Ct. 1389, 152 L. Ed. 2d. 403 (2002). ("The right to think is the beginning of freedom, and speech must be protected from the government because speech is the beginning of thought.")

19. ICCPR, Art. 19.

20. *Genetics and Human Behaviour: The Ethical Context* (London: Nuffield Council on Bioethics, 2002), http://nuffieldbioethics.org/wp-content/uploads/2014/07/Genetics-and-human-behaviour.pdf (emphasis added).

21. See Rafael Yuste, Jared Genser, and Stephanie Herrmann, "It's Time for Neuro-Rights: New Human Rights for the Age of Neurotechnology," *Horizons*, no. 18 (Winter 2021): 158–159, https://www.cirsd.org/files/000/000/008/47/7dc9d3b6165ee497761b0abe69612108833b5cff.pdf.

22. See, for example, Aleš Završnik, "Criminal Justice, Artificial Intelligence Systems, and Human Rights," *ERA Forum* 20 (2020): 567–583, https://doi.org/10.1007/s12027-020-00602-0.

23. Andrew McStay, "The Right to Privacy in the Age of Emotional AI," OCHR Report, https://www.ohchr.org/Documents/Issues/DigitalAge/ReportPrivacyinDigitalAge/AndrewMcStayProfessor%20of%20Digital%20Life,%20BangorUniversityWales UK.pdf.

24. See, for example, Melissa Bateson, Daniel Nettle, and Gilbert Roberts, "Cues of Being Watched Enhance Cooperation in a Real-World Setting," *Biology Letters* 2, no. 3 (2006): 412–414, https://www.ncbi.nlm.nih.gov/pmc/articles/PMC1686213/; Mathias Ekstrom, "Do Watching Eyes Affect Charitable Giving? Evidence from a Field Experiment," *Experimental Economics* 15 (2012): 530–546, https://link.springer.

com/article/10.1007%2Fs10683-011-9312-6; Jiaxin Yu, Philip Tseng, Neil G. Muggleton, and Chi-Hung Juan, "Being Watched by Others Eliminates the Effect of Emotional Arousal on Inhibitory Control," *Frontiers in Psychology* 6, no. 4 (2015), https://www.ncbi.nlm.nih.gov/pmc/articles/PMC4299288.

25. See, for example, Drew Ehlers, "Is Blockchain the Answer for COVID Vaccine Passports?," *Government Technology*, March 31, 2021, https://www.govtech.com /opinion/is-blockchain-the-answer-for-covid-vaccine-passports.html.

26. See, for example, ICCPR, Art. 19; Council of Europe, European Convention on Human Rights (hereafter ECHR) (Strasbourg: Directorate of Information, 1952), Art. 8.

27. Bachelet, "Human Rights in the Digital Age."

28. William F. Schulz and Sushma Raman, *The Coming Good Society: Why New Realities Demand New Rights* (Cambridge, MA: Harvard University Press, 2020), 7, 14.

29. See, for example, Sarah E. Igo, *The Known Citizen: A History of Privacy in Modern America* (Cambridge, MA: Harvard University Press, 2018).

30. UDHR, Art. 12; ICCPR, Art. 17.

31. See Oliver Digglemann and Maria Nicole Cleis, "How the Right to Privacy Became a Human Right," *Human Rights Law Review* 14 (2014), 441–458, https://doi .org/10.1093/hrlr/ngu014.

32. Schulz and Raman, *The Coming Good Society*, 104.

33. See, for example, Martin Tisne, "Collective Data Rights Can Stop Big Tech from Obliterating Privacy," *MIT Technology Review*, May 25, 2021, https://www.technolo gyreview.com/2021/05/25/1025297/collective-data-rights-big-tech-privacy.

34. McStay, "The Right to Privacy in the Age of Emotional AI," 5.

35. See, for example, Woodrow Hartzog and Evan Selinger, "Surveillance as Loss of Obscurity," *Washington and Lee Law Review* 72, no. 3 (Summer 2015): 1343–1388.

36. Jillian C. York, "The Right to Anonymity is Vital to Free Expression: Now and Always," Electronic Frontier Foundation, March 25, 2020, https://www.eff.org /deeplinks/2020/03/right-anonymity-vital-free-expression-now-and-always.

37. See ICCPR, Art. 18; ECHR, Art. 9.

38. See Leonard M. Hammer, *The International Right to Freedom of Conscience* (Farnham, UK: Ashgate, 2001), 34.

39. Schulz and Raman, *The Coming Good Society*, 10.

40. Yuste, Genser, and Herrmann, "It's Time for Neuro-Rights," 155, 160.

41. For example, the Chilean Congress recently amended the Chilean Constitution to specifically recognize rights to physical and mental integrity in relation to the advancement of neurotechnologies, including requirements and conditions for the use of these technologies in people as well as protections for cerebral activity and any data derived from it. See "En histórica votación, aprueban proyecto del ley que regulará los neuroderechos en Chile," *La Tercera*, April 13, 2021, https://www.latercera.com/que-pasa/noticia/en-historica-votacion-aprueban-proyecto-del-ley-que-regulara-los-neuroderechos-en-chile/4IAQJIVHM5F75GRLAR2GQ27V24. Similarly, in July 2021, Spanish president Pedro Sánchez published a new Digital Rights Charter, including articles that specifically address human rights in relation to the application and use of neurotechnologies. See "Carta Derechos Digitales," Gobierno de Espana, July 2021, Art. XXVI, https://www.lamoncloa.gob.es/presidente/activi dades/Documents/2021/140721-Carta_Derechos_Digitales_RedEs.pdf.

42. Jan Christoph Bublitz and Reinhard Merkel, "Crimes against Minds: On Mental Manipulations, Harms and a Human Right to Mental Self-Determination," *Criminal Law and Philosophy* 8, no. 1 (2014): 51–77, https://doi.org/10.1007/s11572-012 -9172-y; Jean-Yves Boire, "On Cognitive Liberty," *Journal of Cognitive Liberties* 22, no. 4 (2001): 195, https://doi.org/10.1016/S1297-9562(01)90048-8; Marcello Ienca and Roberto Andorno, "Towards New Human Rights in the Age of Neuroscience and Neurotechnology," *Life Sciences, Society and Policy* 13, no. 1 (2017): 1–27, https://doi.org/10.1186/s40504-017-0050-1.

43. See, for example, Simon McCarthy-Jones, "The Autonomous Mind: The Right to Freedom of Thought in the Twenty-First Century," *Frontiers in Artificial Intelligence* 2, no. 19 (September 26, 2019), https://doi.org/10.3389/frai.2019.00019.

44. Susie Alegre, "Rethinking Freedom of Thought for the 21st Century," *European Human Rights Law Review* 3 (2017): 222.

45. See Yuste, Genser, and Herrmann, "It's Time for Neuro-Rights," 162–163.

46. See Katie Way, "Workers of the World, Unplug: The Fight for the 'Right to Disconnect,'" *Vice*, October 16, 2019, https://www.vice.com/en/article/evjk4w/right-to -disconnect-legislation-labor-movement.

47. UDHR, Art. 24; ICESCR, Art. 7.

48. See ICESCR, Art. 12, Art. 15.

49. Yuste, Genser, and Herrmann, "It's Time for Neuro-Rights," 161.

50. Through ratification of international human rights instruments such as the ICCPR and ICESCR, ratifying parties undertake to implement domestic measures and legislation in accordance with their treaty obligations and duties. See "International Human Rights Law," UN Office of the High Commissioner for Human

Rights, accessed February 15, 2022, https://www.ohchr.org/en/professionalinterest
/pages/internationallaw.aspx.

51. UN Office of the High Commissioner for Human Rights, *Guiding Principles on
Business and Human Rights: Implementing the United Nations "Protect, Respect and
Remedy" Framework* (New York: United Nations, 2011), Principle II.A.12, https://
www.ohchr.org/documents/publications/guidingprinciplesbusinesshr_en.pdf.
("The responsibility of business enterprises to respect human rights refers to
internationally recognized human rights—understood, at a minimum, as those
expressed in the International Bill of Human Rights and the principles concerning
fundamental rights set out in the International Labour Organization's Declaration
on Fundamental Principles and Rights at Work.")

52. UN Office of the High Commissioner for Human Rights, *Guiding Principles on
Business and Human Rights*, Principle II.A.18. (Human rights due diligence should
also involve undertaking human rights impact assessments using "all internationally recognized human rights as a reference point," including ESCRs).

53. See, for example, Jack Nicas, Raymond Zhong, and Daisuke Wakabayashi,
"Censorship, Surveillance and Profits: A Hard Bargain for Apple in China," *New
York Times*, May 17, 2021, https://www.nytimes.com/2021/05/17/technology/apple
-china-censorship-data.html.

54. See, for example, Elizabeth Brico, "'Privacy Is Becoming a Luxury': What Data
Leaks Are Like for the Poor," *Vice*, March 14, 2019, https://www.vice.com/en
/article/mbz493/privacy-is-becoming-a-luxury-what-data-leaks-are-like-for-the-poor.

55. See UN Committee on Economic, Social, and Cultural Rights, "*General Comment No. 24 (2017) on State Obligations under the International Covenant on Economic,
Social, and Cultural Rights in the Context of Business Activities,*" E/C.12/GC/24, August
10, 2017, paras. 21–22, https://docstore.ohchr.org/SelfServices/FilesHandler.ashx
?enc=4slQ6QSmlBEDzFEovLCuW1a0Szab0oXTdImnsJZZVQcIMOuuG4TpS9jwIhCJ
cXiuZ1yrkMD%2fSj8YF%2bSXo4mYx7Y%2f3L3zvM2zSUbw6ujlnCawQrJx3hlK8Od
ka6DUwG3Y.

56. See UN Office of the High Commissioner for Human Rights, *Guiding Principles
on Business and Human Rights*, Principle I.B.5, Commentary. ("States do not relin-
quish their international human rights law obligations when they privatize the
delivery of services that may impact upon the enjoyment of human rights.")

57. Ian Bogost, "The Internet Is Just Investment Banking Now," *Atlantic*, February
4, 2022, https://www.theatlantic.com/technology/archive/2022/02/future-internet
-blockchain-investment-banking/621480.

58. "Guidelines 04/2020 on the Use of Location Data and Contact Tracing Tools in
the Context of the COVID-19 Outbreak," European Data Protection Board, April 21,

2021, https://edpb.europa.eu/sites/default/files/files/file1/edpb_guidelines_20200420 _contact_tracing_covid_with_annex_en.pdf.

59. "Interim Position Paper: Considerations regarding Proof of COVID-19 Vaccination for International Travelers," World Health Organization, February 5, 2021, https://www.who.int/news-room/articles-detail/interim-position-paper-consider ations-regarding-proof-of-covid-19-vaccination-for-international-travellers.

60. See, for example, Akash Kapur, "The Rising Threat of Digital Nationalism," *Wall Street Journal*, November 1, 2019, https://www.wsj.com/articles/the-rising-threat-of -digital-nationalism-11572620577.

Index